Corporate Memory

Kenneth A. Megill

Corporate Memory

Records and Information Management
in the Knowledge Age

2nd Edition

K · G · Saur München 2005

Bibliographic information published by Die Deutsche Bibliothek
Die Deutsche Bibliothek lists this publication in the Deutsche Nationalbibliografie;
detailed bibliographic data is available in the internet at http://dnb.ddb.de.

⊗

Printed on acid-free paper

Typesetting by Florence Production Ltd., Stoodleigh, Devon, Great Britain.

Printed and bound by Strauss GmbH, Mörlenbach, Germany.

ISBN 3-598-24371-5

The Author

Kenneth A Megill specializes in transforming organizations – and enabling them to manage their information in order to improve the way they do their business. He combines a life of theory and practice with a broad sweep of knowledge and experience. He began his professional career as a philosopher, receiving his doctorate in philosophy at Yale University at the age of 26 after studying two years in Europe. He was a successful teacher and published more than a dozen articles in professional journals of philosophy. In his first book, The New Democratic Theory, published in 1970, he brought his philosophical skills and training to the practical pursuits in which he was involved as a political activist. He went on to be a trade union leader organizing and representing 8,000 faculty and professional employees in the State University System of Florida and moved to Washington, D.C. in 1982 where he continues to live and work. He is a certified records manager, a certified archivist and holds a masters degree in library and information science. He taught in a graduate school in library and information science, but has focused in helping organizations manage the information of value for re-use. He was on the faculty of the School of Library and Information Science at the Catholic University of America in Washington, DC where he directed its Information Resources Management Program. Prior to joining the faculty he was records manager at the Office of the Comptroller of the Currency, a federal agency that serves as the administrator of national banks. He recently led a three year project to create an integrated digital environment for the United States Air Force. He is now working with Scan-Optics, a thirty-five year old manufacturing company that builds high-end scanning equipment, to build a new business line of Knowledge Application Services.

Contents

Chapter 5: Valuing documents   41

Chapter 6: The corporate memory manager   55

Chapter 7: The technologies   73

Preface to Second Edition

Much has happened in the decade since I first conceived this book on Corporate Memory, yet little has changed. Carlos Cuadra and Judy Wanger introduced me to the term "corporate memory," when I was working with them to develop one of the first automated records management software packages. Now corporate memory is a widely accepted and widely used term. It is now most often used in the discussion of "knowledge management" – a term that a decade ago did not exist. Ten years ago even the most optimistic of us underestimated the speed at which technology is changing the way we do our work.

A decade later I have returned, hopefully with a better understanding, to the problem of how an organization can capture, organize, retrieve and re-use the information that it creates. In the Knowledge Age that is developing all around us, the essential evidence[1] of an organization is a valuable resource that is lost or poorly utilized.

Since I wrote the first edition of this book, we now have new terms and words we can use to understand our situation. But the problem I identified in the first edition of this book – the loss of corporate memory – has not been solved. Indeed, a combination of factors, some technological and some social and political, have converged to make the identification, preservation and re-use of corporate memory even more necessary than before.

I have added discussions of three new topics – one on digital archives and one on Knowledge Applications Services and a discussion of ISO Standard 15489 which gives some order to the field of records management. These topics were not on the table when the first edition appeared. I have also changed the subtitle to reflect the fact that this discussion is within the field of records management and that we are, indeed, leaving the Information Age and entering into the Knowledge Age.

The chapter on digital archives is my attempt to link the discussions in the archival community with those in records management. They are clearly one community, even though there is still little practical collaboration. The

---

[1] "Essential evidence" is a term used by the United States National Archives to describe what a record is.

struggle between archivists and records managers has, unfortunately, been primarily waged between those who see valuable information from the viewpoint of history (the archivists) and those who focus on the practical, business uses of information (the records managers).

By talking about digital archives, I believe that the fundamental unity of these two disciplines and crafts can be demonstrated.

The last ten years have given me several opportunities to apply and amplify some of the concepts that I articulated in the first edition of this book. Much of what I have learned is summed up in the modifications I have made in the original text.

I have also published two additional books that deal with topics related to the concepts dealt with in Corporate Memory.

Document Management, which is a collaborative effort with my dear friend and colleague, Herb Schantz, who introduced me to the fascinating and challenging world of capturing data from thousands, hundreds of thousands and even millions of forms and other documents. We were able to take the notion of a document as a verb, which I articulated first in this book, and apply it to a very different technological environment. In the context of document management, a document is the answer to a question, not necessarily a physical object. The technologies and techniques used by document managers can be applied, when understood properly, to virtual digital documents.

My most recent book, Thinking for a Living. The Coming Age of Knowledge Work gave me a chance to return to my first discipline, philosophy, and think through the concepts of knowledge and work in light of the startling technological and social developments of the past half century.

I have, where it made sense, included in this edition references to my other books and changed some terminology. I was surprised, for example, that I included no specific discussion of metadata. My omission of the importance of networks and the Internet are more understandable, since they were just becoming part of our work life as I completed the first edition. Now we live in what some call a Network Centric Environment.

Despite the apparent speed of technological change, the basic argument that I put forward in the first edition is still valid – we need to identify and preserve information of value for reuse: corporate memory.

Introduction

Corporate Memory is information that a corporation (organization or business) creates which is of value for re-use. This book is written for the corporate memory manager of the future. Information managers in the knowledge age will come from different professions that are in the process of merging. I do not argue that such integration should take place: I just assume that it is. I try to point out practical ways in which the information of an organization can be managed in the electronic age.

I come to this activity as a professional records manager who, like most records managers, had a previous career. I began my professional life as a philosopher and moved on to the world of organizations and politics before coming to information management. My roots show in this discussion, which I hope will be a contribution to the development of a systematic theory for information management. My work with many organizations has convinced me that many, if not most, of the problems of organizations and businesses are information problems, and if we can find practical ways to identify and preserve the memory of the organizations in which we work, our lives will be not only more efficient but also fuller.

Two colleagues, Carlos A. Cuadra and Judith Wanger, encouraged me to develop a coherent theory for managing information in the electronic age. Carlos wrote a paper a few years ago entitled 'The Corporate Memory and the Bottom Line', suggesting that managing wordprocessed documents would begin to bring electronic documents under control. When he asked me to look at a draft of that paper, I recognized that he had pointed the way to solutions for many problems facing records management in the electronic age. Some of the material in this book is taken directly from Carlos' original paper. He has also used his extensive editorial skills to help make this work more intelligible.

At about that same time I began working with Judith Wanger, Vice-President of Cuadra Associates, to develop an application for the STAR software package. STAR is a text-based database application developed by Cuadra Associates that I had used in my work as a records manager for a federal agency. When we began to develop the application, I tried to elaborate on the work of records management and identify how to automate its essential activities. Six months later Judith was able to show me an application that managed records from cradle to grave, without regard to the media in which they are stored.

I was attracted to records management in 1987 as an emerging profession of information management that focused on throwing things away in a timely and orderly manner. Establishing disposition schedules – the heart of traditional records management – was the primary tool used to bring records under control. In about 1992, a shift in the attitudes of the profession became apparent. One reason for this was the arrival of image technology as a usable and cost-effective tool for records management. The other was the development of wordprocessing in a networked environment.

With the arrival of imaging, wordprocessing and networking technologies, most records were no longer kept on paper. Rather, they were created and stored in electronic form. Thus a convergence of imaging, wordprocessing and networking enables offices to move records from place to place electronically without copying them on paper. Paper copies became copies of records, not the records themselves.

Many other people have helped me with this project. Most of all, I want to thank the many students who stimulated me to develop a theory for records and information management that will meet the needs of the next century. Leonard Mignerey, whom I worked with when he was MIS Director at Catholic University, introduced me to the world of management information systems and showed me how the world of data and the world of records are colliding. Most of the ideas in the chapter on the 'new document' came out of discussions with him and other colleagues in an informal seminar in 1995.

Barry Wheeler, my former colleague at Catholic University, who is now working to create the digital library at the Library of Congress. During the time I was writing the first edition, he was the engineer next door who patiently explained how to use the new tools that constantly arrive.

At the time I was writing the first edition, he insisted that I move to Windows even though I had just barely begun to manage the strange world of DOS. Since then he has worked with me through many lunches where we mused over new technologies and how to make them really useful. Barry also showed me the difference between training and learning, and convinced me that in order for technology to be used anywhere, we needed to develop new ways to bring it into our lives. Noel Dickover later showed me how Performance Centered Learning can be done.

Sheryl K. Rosenthal worked with me to develop my first records management database at the Comptroller of the Currency in 1988. When I worked as a consultant to Cuadra Associates, she invited me to several demonstrations of STAR software to potential clients who helped me think through the requirements of automated records management and archival applications. As a teacher of online searching, she helped me understand the power of this technology and, when I wrote this book, as Manager of Research Systems at the Washington Post, she helped me understand the application of searching technologies in an information-intensive environment. In her current position at the US News and World Report she continues to make practical use of technologies described here to make information accessible to those who need it.

Herb Schantz introduced me to the notions of workflow and showed its integral relationship with imaging technology and its relationship to document management. Dr. Letty Schantz did a careful editing job of the first edition that was particularly helpful. Herb and I went on to collaborate on a book on Document Management and our professional lives have been intertwined ever since.

In addition, a large number of students, friends and colleagues made comments on various drafts of the book. These include (but are not limited to) Clay Cochrane, Fred Jordan, Deanna Marcum, Bob Nawrocki, Fred Stielow and Betsy Woods (who also assisted with the indexing). Finally, I must thank my partner of twenty years, Lawrence Tan, for his patience, understanding and support. As a businessman and accountant, he tried to make this philosopher as practical as he could make him.

For the second edition, in addition to those mentioned above, several of whom took the time to read the revised copy, I am gratefully to Deb Marshall, Marilyn Barth, Dean Harris, Rebecca Weiner, Evie Lotze, Bill Larsen, John Latham and Susan Brown for their assistance.

Kenneth Megill
Knowledge Application Services
Washington, D.C.

CHAPTER ONE

Empowerment

The information revolution (i.e. making it possible for new things to happen), at its best is about empowerment. Like all empowering forces, information is a tool that can be used for many purposes. It can enslave people. If information is controlled and shaped, people can be made to act in what seem to be strange ways: they buy new and useless products; they vote against what appears to be their best interests; they believe what appears to be false. Yet information is also an empowering force: it enables people to know and understand the situation they are in. We are awash with information and are faced with a situation in which there is too much to know and so little understanding.

This book is about managing information in the knowledge age. The technology that enables the knowledge age is the computer, a tool that is based on a simple choice: is something on or off? Is it yes or no? The genius of the computer is that it enables us to compute rapidly. It takes away much of what we used to do – counting and calculating. It gives us the possibility of understanding because it takes away many of the tasks that we once thought were so important and makes them routine. It makes it possible for work to focus on making knowledge – justified true belief – the answer to the question, "Is it a good idea to . . .?"

As the technology develops, the possibility for liberation and empowerment is built. The change in the way in which information is produced, used, and managed is profoundly changing the nature of the organizations in which we work.

Information as a resource

Information has always been important: those who knew what was going on had power over those who did not. The chancellor of the royal court was often the person who was able to read, and functioned as the keeper of the Seal. This person controlled information by deciding what would become an official document and what would not. Information was power and the ability to know was power.

Now, however, we think of information as not just an important tool, but as a resource to be managed.[2] In the electronic age information is an asset that can be managed like other assets. Money, people, land and natural resources have long been assets. If you had money, you had power. If you had people you could dominate the land. If you had territory and lived in a land of milk and honey you had power. Your assets enabled you to have power, and power was the ability to use and manage assets. In the Information Age, information was an asset and therefore power. It empowered corporations with it to do things that corporations without it could not do.

Information is now generally recognized as an asset. Like other resources, information can be created, stored, kept and used. It can be sold and traded.

And it can be used and reused.

Using information is a little different from using other resources. When land is used for one purpose, it cannot normally be used for another. When personnel resources are being used to doing one thing, then they cannot usually do something else. When money is taken from your bank account to pay a bill, there is less in the account. Most resources are diminished when they are used.

Information, however, is different. Shared information is not lost. In fact, information often loses value if it is not used – by the owner/creator and by others. When information is shared and put into context, it often gains value for the creator as well as for the person with whom it is shared.

Information is not only not a depletable resource, it is one that grows and thrives with use.

---

2   See Megill,Kenneth A, et.al. Making the Information Revolution. A Handbook for Federal Information Resource Managers. Washington: Association for Information and Image Management 1996.

The demise of command structures

Corporations are, by and large, established in order to manage scarce resources. They operate from the top down in a structure in which one person commands and allocates resources. Control of the budget, the ultimate resource of the corporation, means power.

The strain on the modern corporation created by the impact of information technology is just beginning. Like any technology, information technology holds within it the possibility for enslavement and control as well as liberation and empowerment. Under a social order, characterized by hierarchical and command-driven organizations, information is used as a means of control.

Information cannot be managed like money or other resources since information grows and prospers in an environment in which it is shared[3] used and reused, the better an organization is able to share its information, the more valuable that information becomes. The more information can be reused, the greater its value becomes, for information gains value in context with other information.

The memory of an organization is one of its greatest assets and one that the traditional hierarchical organization is badly equipped to manage. In order to utilize information to the fullest, it needs to be shared and dispersed, not hoarded and doled out. Like other resources, information needs to be organized so that it can be retrieved and used. Unlike other resources, it is not diminished with use.

In order to manage information resources effectively, a new kind of corporation is developing. The traditional organizational structure based on command from the top and obedience at the bottom is transforming into one that rewards and encourages ingenuity and openness. The ability

> "Collaboration is a creative process that emerges out of a common desire to achieve a goal. Collaboration takes place when we all play the same game, with the same goals and a common understanding of what the game is about."
>
> Megill, Thinking for a Living, p. 53.

---

[3] Sharing is used in the sense of collaboration, which is a two-way street. Sharing is not synonymous with a one-way giving away of information.

to analyze becomes more important than the ability to follow directions. Information can be effectively reused if people are empowered. They need to have access to information, which must be organized so that it is available and can be retrieved quickly and easily. Not only must workers be empowered to get at specific pieces of information, they need to be able to browse through the corporate memory in order to understand a subject.

Recycling

Recycling is a part of everyday life. We know that if we are to survive as a planet and as a society, then we need to manage our environment with care. We need to replenish our resources, not simply deplete them. Information is one of our most valuable resources, yet it is generally created over and over again, at great cost to those who make up the ranks of information workers. Just as the rise of mass production made it possible to produce farm products and industrial goods more efficiently, so the invention and mass application of computing power makes it possible for the management of information to be more effective and efficient.

The management of corporate memory is a task of recycling information. It requires the identification of information that is created for one purpose but may also be used for another. It requires seeing information as not just a product of a particular department or business unit of an organization, but as a product that belongs to the entire organization. Instead of being the property of the person or department that created it, information belongs to the corporation – the organization as a whole – and needs to be managed as one of the organization's valuable resources.

Browsing and retrieving

Too often information is viewed as simply an item that can be picked up and put into another place. The true value of information, however, is often found in the context in which it is created and used. Taking it out of that context can sometimes destroy its value, whereas putting it in another context can often enhance its value. Often the most valuable information is found in unexpected places. A properly managed corporate memory system enables us to discover the unexpected.

The information worker needs the power and the ability to browse through the corporate memory in order to see what information might be valuable in unexpected ways. Browsing can only be done by someone who is familiar with a subject and is seeking to expand his or her understanding.

The classic act of browsing is standing in front of a shelf full of books and seeing what else there is about the subject that might be interesting. Such browsing is possible because library books are arranged together with others on the same topic so that users can not only find the specific book that is required, but also expand their understanding of the topic being investigated. That browsing pales when we have corporate memory systems with retrieval systems that deliver us the unexpected.

A new soul

The first stage of the information revolution, the increasing of production and the flattening of organizations, is well under way. The groundwork for the next stage is developing. This is the stage of liberation and empowerment. The soul of the new corporation will emerge when the information worker can combine knowledge of the business with the ability to make decisions. The mediating power of middle management will no longer be needed in the new corporation. The function of these managers to receive, process and pass on information, will become increasingly irrelevant as information technology develops. The ability to make decisions will belong to those meeting customer needs, and the manager will become a liberator and coordinator.

The Knowledge Age

Work in the Age of Knowledge is . . . largely the production of knowledge. As we enter this Knowledge Age, our work takes on very different characteristics than the work we do in an industrial environment. In this new age, in order for work to be done most efficiently, we will not be paid for our work time, but for what we know and what we get done.

Megill, Thinking for a Living, p. 54

CHAPTER TWO

The memory problem

An organization can no longer rely on traditional ways of keeping its corporate memory. In the past, the memory of an organization was kept in paper documents and in the collective memory of its employees, but these ways are now obsolete. As a result of the information revolution and corporate downsizing the ways of doing business are changing, and today the memory of an organization is increasingly housed in electronic form.

Corporate memory consists of the active and historical information in an organization that is worth sharing, managing and preserving for later reuse. The concept of corporate memory is not limited to commercial organizations: we use the term 'corporate' to mean 'total' or 'organizational'.

Businesses, government agencies, educational institutions, nonprofit research institutes and other types of organizations have essential information that should be safeguarded, able to be retrieved on demand and reused. Such organizations may prefer to think in terms of an institutional memory, but the concept is the same.

Corporate and organizational culture is changing in fundamental ways to alter the relationship between staff members and the corporation. Employees seldom spend their entire career with a single organization: They move from place to place. Most corporations no longer prize long service. Organizations undergo fundamental transformations that make employees superfluous and, as a result, the carriers of corporate memory are eliminated.

The corporate memory of a given institution may be embedded in millions of documents, all of which might become endangered by loss or mismanagement. Over the years several attempts have been made to define the quantity of information produced and the effects of increasing storage capacities on managing the memory of an organization.

The proliferation of documents and copies of documents in an organization is a major cause of the loss of corporate memory. An equally important cause is a significant change in corporate management. Instead of one or two changes of leadership in 10 years we are seeing three or four. Instead of one or two crises in the organization, such as a major lawsuit, we are seeing many more. As a result, those who carry the corporate memory of the organization disappear as the tenure of staff and officials shortens.

Today, the availability of shared file servers encourages users to maintain multiple copies or near-copies on their personal computers, in various shared spaces and as attachments to e-mails. The servers become the electronic equivalent of the communal refrigerator, complete with unidentifiable fossils lurking in the corners. Storing a potentially damaging item of information after its useful or legally mandated life may cost only a few pennies or dollars per month, but if the item is subpoenaed and used against the organization, such needless retention can be costly.

The cost of keeping too much corporate memory

In the paper era, when the organization faced a crisis (such as a lawsuit, for example) it often relied on records that were kept in the basement. Retrieval of information stored in the basement depended on the knowledge of staff that had been with the organization for a long time. When the leadership of the organization changed, records managers were often called in to sort out the paper records. Keeping inactive records in the basement in this way worked fairly well because they were on paper and, if found, could be still be read. Also, since records from the same office or related offices were normally stored together, it was often possible to get the information needed even if a particular document was not available or had been destroyed. Mildew or water might have damaged some of the records, but the information needed might be found in others stored nearby.

Now, however, with most information stored in various digital forms (in addition to paper in many cases) the task of piecing together evidence of what happened after the fact is compounded. The volatility and complexity of corporate memory repositories demands a way to manage corporate memory in a digital environment.

Box 2.1 Endangered memory

It is difficult to quantify the loss of memory. The first edition of this book, written a decade ago, contains the following attempts to quantify memory. The trends identified here have, no doubt, continued:

Eighty percent of corporate electronic information is in documents, as opposed to structured database records.[1]

Estimates of the number of documents produced each year in the United States alone include:

- 100 billion documents with an average of 19 copies of each business document.[2]
- 320 billion documents per year in the United States alone.[3]
- 92 billion documents per year.[4]

The capacities of the typical PC network will grow from 7.2 Gb in 1993 to 41 Gb by 1997. When you consider that the average 5 Gb of network data contain 500,000 files, how will anyone be able to manage the number of files on these networks as they double each year?[5]

Network data storage requirements are increasing at an estimated 60–100% per year. Given that trend, some analysts predict that the average local area network will require more than 50 GB of storage within the next couple of years.[6]

'The average user has enough trouble creating directories or structuring files into folders, much less remembering later where he or she has put files. The inadequacies of contemporary file systems have never been more apparent, nor the need for powerful document management tools greater.'[7]

---

[1] From a report by Peripheral Strategies, cited in Aardvark (July 1994).
[2] From a study by the Gartner Group, cited in Modern Office Technology (April 1992).
[3] A 1991 report citing Fujitsu data cited in Computer Reseller News (May 20, 1991).
[4] From a study by Xerox, AIIM and the Gartner Group, cited by John Dykeman in Modern Office Technology (April 1992).
[5] Frank Gilbane, editor of "The Gilbane Report on Open Information and Document Systems," cited in Byte (August 1994).
[6] Jordahl, Gregory 'Hierarchical Storage Management: A Solution to Skyrocketing Data Management Costs.' Inform. Association of Information and Image Management International (AIIM). (X,2) Feb 1996, pp. 29–32.
[7] Andy Reinhard, 'Managing the New Document,' Byte (August 1994).

The cost of losing corporate memory

The loss of information from corporate memory can be very costly, no matter how it is stored. Estimates of the cost of lost or misplaced information are difficult to make, but some attempts to quantify these costs can be made.

In addition to the expense caused by staff time spent searching for lost documents, when a staff member needs information that is not readily available entire operations may stop while that information is sought or recreated. The result is a dramatic increase in cost caused by the failure of the organization to set up adequate information management systems. Such failure can also expose the organization to litigation losses, owing to the inability to find relevant documents when needed, or to the forced disclosure of documents and other data that were not properly destroyed in a timely manner.

The widespread use of wordprocessing software eases the creation of documents, and most users have the ability to download almost unlimited numbers of documents at very little cost. Ineffective management here can lead to unnecessary capital expenditure on hardware and network servers, in order to store documents that may no longer be useful.

The proliferation of information technology is revolutionizing the way organizations and corporations function. The volume of information that is available and accessible is increasing dramatically. We need to invent ways to make the corporate memory available throughout the organization.

Causes of lost memory

Information is lost to the organization when it can no longer be retrieved for use. Some possible ways to lose corporate memory include premature discarding, not throwing things away in a timely manner, forgetting where something is put, not having adequate documentation or losing the medium on which the memory is stored.

Premature discarding

Information can be lost when disks or files are accidentally erased or when a note or piece of paper that appears to have no value is thrown away. Most organizations have ways to minimize the danger of accidentally losing information in electronic form. Multiple copies of documents and files are

Box 2.2 The cost of lost information

The following data, from a decade ago, are still valid:

- One estimate is that a user working in Windows spends an average of 7% of their working time looking for files.[1]
- According to one source, in 1991 the average cost of a misfiled record was $126.81.[2] This figure refers to a paper record, but we might assume that the cost of a misfiled electronic record may be equally as great.
- Large organizations lose a document every 12 seconds.[3]
- 7.5% of all paper documents are lost forever, and active files are growing at the rate of 25% per year.[4]
- U.S. managers spend an average of three hours a week (four weeks a year) on a paper chase searching for misfiled, mislabeled or lost papers.[5]
- According to some estimates, executives spend an average of 150–200 hours a year looking for misplaced, misfiled or lost documents.
- One estimate is that three percent of all documents are incorrectly filed.[6]

---

[1] Tyrone Butler, president of the Association of Records Managers and Administrators, ARMA Conference, Toronto, September 1994.

[2] The Records and Retrieval Report. The Newsletter for Professional Information Managers. Greenwood Publishing Group, Westport, CT, Volume 8, Number 4, April 1992, p. 10. This issue is written by Robert N Allerding, a Certified Records Manager and is entitled "The Cost of Managing Information. This authoritative publication gives the costs of a misfiled record from 1975 to 1991, as well as the average cost of filing per inch ($14.88), cost of records stored in active files per file drawer ($11,585.53) and other costs.

Unfortunately, there is no indication how the figures were derived and using an exact figure, to the penny, makes the data suspect.

[3] Byte (August 1994).

[4] From a 1987 Coopers and Lybrand Study, cited in Puget Sound Business Journal (February 11, 1994).

[5] From a Survey by Acountemps, cited in Working Woman (1986).

[6] Cited in Modern Office Technology (April 1992).

circulated widely. Data are backed up electronically and/or additional paper copies are printed out. Making copies has become the first line of defense against the loss of corporate memory. Even if a document is discarded it can often be reconstructed, since information is kept in a number of different versions and on different media.

Not throwing things away in a timely manner

Evidence of what actually happened, which version was used by whom and for what purpose is lost in the jumble of documents and e-mails and makes it nearly impossible to answer the question, "Why did we do that?" In a digital environment more problems are caused by not discarding material in an orderly way than through premature discarding.

Managing the corporate memory does not mean simply saving things forever, but also throwing things out. A major cause of the loss of corporate memory is keeping too many documents and too many versions of documents, which makes it difficult to determine the meaning and significance of a particular record. Documents are often kept without deciding whether they are valuable. A corporate memory system must not only preserve documents, but must also preserve information about how the document was used, who had access to it, and its relationship to other documents.

Forgetting where it is

Systems to prevent inadvertent or deliberate discarding of information are relatively widespread. What is much more difficult to prevent is losing information because we cannot remember where we put it. We know it is somewhere: retrieving it is the problem.

Information can be lost in an electronic environment for several reasons.

1. The way in which the information is stored may not be designed for retrieval through browsing and searching: many electronic systems require the user to remember specific file names in order to retrieve information. In order to manage electronic information, it is also necessary to be able to search for specific information that exists, as well as to be able to browse to find unexpected information. Losing electronic information is often the result of poorly designed systems that do not support retrieval through searching and browsing.
2. Another reason information is lost is that it has been changed or modified so that it is not where one would reasonably expect it to be. Of course, this may also happen in paper-based systems, but it is much more common in electronic systems where material can be quickly and easily moved and copied. In order to find lost information it is often

necessary to know the history of the document: who had it, who copied it, where it might be located now, for whom they are valuable and whether they have value for re-use.[4]

3. A third reason information may be lost is that the searcher has the wrong picture of what is being looked for. In the paper world we often look for the red book or the fat file or the 'addendum to the report sent in last year to support the budget'. These pictures of information and containers of information help us find material. (Color coding files is one way of helping us make pictures of information. A well-designed color-coded filing system enables a user to find information quickly, and it also helps eliminate misfiling, because a file out of place does not fit into the picture. Frequently used reference books are often kept together by size or color, not by subject.) Pictures can be conceptual, as well as physical. In electronic systems the link between information and containers and physical objects is broken, so it is much harder to picture what we are looking for.

Electronic filing systems are not often maintained by people who are trained and held responsible for the quality of their work as filing managers. Filing is generally the responsibility of the file creator, who must be able to retrieve what he or she files. This works relatively well for individuals, but very poorly for organizations where work is increasingly done by project teams.

In an organizational setting misfilings become increasingly harmful, since the lost information may be of interest not to the person who created it, but to others in the organization. Compounding the problem of misfiling is that the number of files in networked situations increases rapidly. An office worker commonly maintains hundreds of electronic files at a workstation, in addition to the thousands of files kept elsewhere in the company. Automating the filing process to enable the creator to register files within a reliable electronic records filing system is a part of establishing a corporate memory management system.

In a typical business situation there are many versions of documents floating around, sometimes in different software packages. Personalized filing systems maintained by those who create and acquire information compound the problem. A corporate memory system is managed and maintained to preserve the corporate memory until it is needed.

---

[4] The technical terms for this, used by archivists, is provenance. Just as we need to know the provenance of an art work to assess its value, so too the provenance of documents assists us in determining their meaning and value.

> **Box 2.3 An example of losing corporate memory**
> One information organization that began an early retirement program discovered when it wanted to modify its major software, that key parts of it were not documented in sufficient detail to make the modifications. None of the staff members who designed or documented the original code still worked for the company. The organization had to seek out retired staff members and bring them back as consultants. Fortunately, the loss was recognized shortly after the departure of the staff members, so the corporate memory could be recovered.

Lack of documentation

Failure to document the actions of an organization is sometimes deliberate, especially at times when major decisions are being made that require strict confidentiality. More often it is simply a matter of not having procedures in place to take minutes or record important conversations. This lack of documentation is not a new problem but is often compounded in an electronic environment, where more informal ways of sharing work are possible than in formal meetings.

Developing a plan to document the activities of an organization needs to be a part of the corporate memory plan. The best time to capture corporate memory is when an activity begins and the best corporate memory systems are a part of the normal business procedures. It is always much more difficult to document after the fact.

Loss of media

Another major reason for the loss of memory is loss of the medium on/in which it is stored. The advent of electronically stored information makes information more fragile. Paper, for all its faults, is a fairly stable medium for storing information. Acidic paper made since 1900 lasts about 50 years. Paper made prior to that time has a much longer life.

Copies made using carbon paper barely last 10 years; thermal fax paper deteriorates within a year or two.

The problem has increased with the electronic storage of records. Software undergoes new revisions about once a year. Even if the information in previous versions may be recoverable, after three or four revisions it becomes increasingly difficult. One software package replaces another and unless there is expensive conversion, records are lost. Operating systems come and go as a result of changing technical capa-

---

Box 2.4 Near loss of 1960 census

One of the classic examples of loss of memory caused by a change in medium is the near loss of the 1960 census in the United States.

The constitution of the United States requires an enumeration of the population every 10 years. In 1960, computers were used for the first time to manage the data gathered. Such a massive undertaking is a logical application for computers.

As the years passed computer technology changed rapidly and it was discovered, to the surprise and horror of the data managers, that there were only two computers that could read the original data, one in the Smithsonian Museum and the other in Japan. Fortunately the data could be migrated to a new machine and the information was saved.

Everyone involved with computers can give a personal example of the loss of data when a new computer, a new processing system or a new program came out. Generally it is fairly easy to save data close to the time when it was created. Over time, however, the difficulty and the cost of converting data increase.

The migration of historical data is one of the major problems in the electronic age. In some respects it is no different from the problems faced by librarians when it was discovered that a change in paper making around the turn of the century meant that much of the printed material literally burns up in a few decades. As a result, much of the information printed on acidic paper is vanishing, never to be recovered, a result of "improved" technologies in the making of paper.

---

bilities, successful marketing and changes in what is thought to be fashionable. Similarly, hardware is undergoing rapid changes. Eight inch and 5.25″ floppy disks have all but disappeared, along with the drives to access them. C.D.'s may be the next storage medium to come and go. This combination of changing software and hardware exacerbates the loss of corporate memory. Spanning two or more generations of technology is a problem that most enterprises do not yet deal with effectively. The evolving nature of data storage and retrieval is adding to the complexity of the problem

We cannot rely on technology to solve the problem of corporate memory management. The "solution" to corporate memory management is not a software package, but developing ways to work that take advantage of the capabilities of the very technologies that make capturing corporate memory so difficult.

> **Box 2.5 Cost of recreating information**
>
> One major European pharmaceutical firm found it was wasting the expensive time of PhD chemists and legal specialists by having them prepare careful, properly documented and legally reviewed responses to inquiries that had in all probability been researched and responded to for a previous inquiry. By having software written to capture, organize and store these responses for a later retrieval, the waste was sharply reduced.

The price of lost information

Lost information can be recovered either by finding it or by recreating it. If the information is available in a file drawer or on a disk drive, an effort can be made to find it. Since searching the contents of file drawers, folders and disk drives is very labor-intensive, this method of recovery can be prohibitively expensive, but the organization may have to accept the cost if a needed document is unique and irreplaceable. For example, a signed contract, agreement, or work order may be so valuable that a manual search is justified.

Searching for files on one or more computer disks requires a different kind of labor. Of course, the possibility of finding the lost information increases if it has been indexed and categorized at the time of creation. The corporate memory management systems we will be discussing later are based on the principle of indexing and categorizing at the time of creation.

Another way to recover lost information is to recreate it. Whether this is a credible alternative depends on several factors, including the availability of appropriate background data and/or access to the staff member or members who originally created the information. Even if the original documents may never be found, the essential information might be recovered.

The cost of creating a business letter is estimated at $10.26 (The Records and Retrieval Report, op.cit., p. 9). The cost of recreating it will vary widely, depending on the complexity of the document and the staff skills required. In most organizations the clerical staff's keyboarding time is a relatively minor part of the cost: the major costs are for the time of the scientific, technical, legal, educational or other staff required to recreate the document.

No matter how we look at it, the cost of not having a corporate memory system can be great, although the problem of lost or misplaced memory increases in an electronic environment. For an organization, a corporate memory management system makes good business sense. It is also critical for the survival of an organization in an electronic environment.

CHAPTER THREE

The corporate memory and Records Management

Corporate memory is information an organization produces that is of value for re-use. Records are "information created, received, and maintained by an organization or a person, in pursuance of legal obligation or in the transaction of business."[5] A record is evidence of what happened. Corporate memory is a broader term and incorporates records – since evidence is kept for someone to use.

Records, however, are often not kept for an organization to use – in fact evidence is generally for someone else – a regulatory agency, a lawyer, a historian or an auditor who wants or needs to know what happened and, perhaps, why it happened.

One of the most significant recent events in the field of records management was the adoption of a standard for records management. This standard emphasizes the importance of records for business and says that records should be managed "to meet current and future business needs by retaining information covering past and present decisions and activities as part of the corporate memory."

The standard correctly identifies corporate memory as more than records and sees that records are one part of that memory. Preserving records (evidence) of a corporate memory management system, but is not, by itself, sufficient to manage corporate memory.

---

[5] This definition comes fro ISO Standard 15489.

To some, the problem of saving corporate memory in the electronic age seems easy to solve: the organization simply gets more disk space. More space is a logical first solution to keeping corporate memory. Just as we once thought that if we got a bigger filing room we would be able to keep and find what we needed, so today we feel that if we get more disks we can keep everything that we need.

The more we keep, the more important it is to have good retrieval mechanisms. The decrease in the cost of electronic storage means that far more data are kept in the course of doing business. As the volume of data increases, the need for good retrieval mechanisms becomes even more obvious.

Even if the cost of storing data electronically continues to drop, we will need to decide what to keep and what to discard. As information becomes electronic, the number of records and potential records increases and the necessity for retrieval systems becomes even greater.

What should be part of the corporate memory?

As indicated earlier, the corporate memory consists of all the active and historical information in an organization that is worth sharing, managing

---

Box 3.1 Exploding number of records

When the Environmental Protection Agency of the US federal government began to develop systems to document electronic data transfer, it became obvious that the number of records needed to document a transaction had soared. Electronic data transmission was introduced in the agency to allow corporations to provide reports and information directly to the agency in electronic form. The savings for both the companies and the agency were obvious. Determining how to document the records was not so obvious.

In a paper environment a report is submitted as a clearly defined object that can be received and tracked. In an electronic environment, a similar report consists of a series of transactions between receiver and sender. In order to document the transaction completely a number of records are created, some of which need to be kept for a short period of time and some of which need to become a part of the report itself.

Finally, in order to use the report it is necessary to be able to recall it in a usable format. As formats and programs change, the amount of data that must be kept along with the actual information in the report increases.

and preserving for reuse. The concept of the corporate memory developed before recorded history, when information was passed orally from generation to generation. Each older generation told the 'tribal history' to the younger generation to ensure that traditions survival techniques and other important information was not lost.

The ancient retelling of the tribal history has its counterpart in modern-day business, where new staff members are introduced to the methods, procedures, rules and traditions of the organization. Although many organizations try to systematize, simplify and document their procedures, most on-the-job training continues to be oral. Although information vital to an organization's operation may not be documented formally in a manual of procedures, it may be embodied in the correspondence, memos and other documents created or received by the organization's employees, and could be used to introduce a new employee to the corporate memory if the relevant documents could be identified and found.

Many organizations are critically dependent on the knowledge of a few key people to keep their corporate memory. If these people leave, the

---

Box 3.2 Contents of the corporate memory

Advertising copy	Newspaper clippings
Analytical techniques	Overhead transparencies
Architectural and engineering	Patents
drawings	Photographs and slides
Art/museum artifacts	Plans
Board, commission and committee	Policies and directives
minutes	Press releases
Briefings and presentations	Proposals
Contracts and other legal documents	Regulations
correspondence	Reports
Directives	Reprints
Electronic bulletin boards, discussion	Resumes
groups etc.	Standards and specifications
Financial records	Summaries of transactions
Ideas	Tables of data in relational
Instructions and instruction manuals	databases
Laboratory and research notes	Technical documentation
Library catalogs	Technical reports
Market/competitive information	Transaction reports
Memos	Videotapes and films
Monographs	Wordprocessed files

organization loses access to much of that corporate memory. The penalties for reliance on oral, non-documented information have been dramatically revealed during the downsizing that is sweeping across organizations around the world. As senior and middle staff members take early retirement or are moved out of the organization, much of the corporate memory goes with them. When the downsizing process breaks the chain of oral history, part of the corporate memory is lost forever. Unfortunately, downsizing often also results in a reduction of the traditional support activities associated with record keeping.

Contents of corporate memory

Corporate memory is one of the organization's most important assets. It encompasses all of the many types of documented and undocumented information that organizational units require to function effectively. This information is used throughout the organization, from executive management through the finance, legal and personnel departments, to those involved in the engineering, manufacturing and marketing activities.

Much of the corporate memory is normally reflected in documents that consist of information packages which are products of the work of the organization. These packages come in many forms: they may be reports, letters, electronic mail messages or databases. They may contain elements stored throughout the organization in various media. Later we will look more closely at the new document that is one of the results of the electronic age.[6]

Each organizational unit needs and uses some or all of these information packets to do its work. Where information packets do not exist, such as when important ideas, concepts or events are not documented, then there is a need to create documents that can be shared. The corporate memory of the organization consists of the sum total of these information packets, whether or not they currently exist, and the history of their use. The most important records that make up the corporate memory are often the transaction reports and the summaries of transactions that deal with the business of the organization. Such reports of activities can often be the basis for all other information.

---

[6] This list, as well as much of the discussion of the concept of corporate memory, is taken from a paper written in 1994 by Carlos A. Cuadra and distributed by Cuadra Associates, called The Corporate Memory and the Bottom Line.

One essential element of the corporate memory that is missing from the list of information packets is the staff of the organization, those who carry the accumulated experience with them. People can provide information and direct us to other information. Indeed some of the items on the list, such as library catalogs and indexes, do not themselves contain information but rather point us towards it.

What should not be part of the corporate memory

Anything that is not worth keeping for reuse does not belong in the corporate memory. Much useful information falls into this category. Being useful once does not make something a part of the corporate memory. Information is often used once and then not needed again, or it is used only by a single person, or it is private. Other information merely serves an audit purpose, to let you know what went wrong if you do not receive a particular message. The long notes at the end of a message sent over the Internet are of this kind. Once the message arrives satisfactorily, the information on the trail may not be necessary. In addition, behind every electronic transaction is a host of transactions that ordinarily need not be saved, once the information is delivered and verified. But sometimes this information might be important. Deciding what is and is not valuable for re-use is an important part of the task of establishing a corporate memory system. In sheer volume, much of the information that organizations create and require may fall within this category that need not be kept for re-use. By identifying these types of information, we can go a long way towards preserving the information storage space of an organization. Judgment is required to decide which information should be part of corporate memory and which should not. Items that may not be worth saving include:

- purely personal information;
- copies of information kept elsewhere;
- some drafts and versions of documents;
- some copies of published materials.

Purely personal information

In theory, all information that an employee uses or produces while at work belongs to the organization. From time to time it may be necessary for a supervisor to press the claim of ownership for all information. A wise staff member will be judicious when using company materials for non-company purposes, whether it is supplies or information resources. Many employees do not look upon electronic mail or other electronic tools in the same way that they do company equipment or supplies that they would not normally even think about using for their personal activities.

In practice, a wise supervisor and a wise company encourage an environment in which a worker feels comfortable. This involves allowing the judicious use of papers, pens, telephones and electronic mail for personal business. As electronic tools enable work to be carried out at home, the distinction between corporate and private activities blurs even more. A creative work environment is one in which space is given for an employee to make judgments about how time is spent and to focus on production rather than simply logging in time.

Some information used by individual workers is idiosyncratic, produced solely for the use of a particular person. This might include things such as notes to buy a gift for a loved one, lunch with a friend and other items that do not concern the corporation. Different people have different work styles: some keep notes and appointments on a computer; others keep them in a diary. Others may have a secretary to do this for them. Unless there is a need to keep such information, which is rarely the case, then that information need not be put into the corporate memory. A good information system allows for differing styles of work, and the peculiarities of a particular person's work style should be respected. It is possible to design systems that capture the information that will become important to the organization without sweeping up purely personal information or limiting the way a staff member works. Capturing corporate memory should facilitate work, not inhibit it.

Other examples of private material that should not be part of the corporate memory are notes, drafts and other preliminary work done by a staff member. Although this is normally the property of the organization, it makes good sense for the staff member to keep such materials until it is time for it to become a part of the corporate memory. Until a draft is shared, it is normally still the "personal" property of the individual and not a part of corporate memory.

Another example of information that should not become a part of the corporate memory is unsolicited material that comes into an office. Most of this can be disposed of by the receiving individual, although some may be of value and be made part of the corporate memory for later use. Again, the principle of treating unsolicited information as private until the staff member uses it or shares it makes good business sense and protects the sense of space that makes an organization a good place to work.

Copies

Copies of information maintained by others need not be part of the corporate memory. A major advantage of developing a reliable corporate information system is that it eliminates the necessity of keeping copies of everything one might need at a future date. It makes little sense to use valuable resources to keep everything in the corporate memory 'just in case' it might be needed.

Proliferating copies is a major cause of data overload and exploding filing systems – in both paper and electronic form. Instead of developing adequate filing systems to preserve information, multiple copies are made and distributed. By identifying which information is a copy and which is not, substantial savings can be made.

A corporate memory management system needs to include ways to decide which organizational unit is responsible for maintaining items that are part of the corporate memory. In records management terms this is called the office of record, and is often the office that initiates the record. Sometimes one office may initiate and copy information for distribution, while another maintains that information for the corporation and becomes the office of record. Even though it is sometimes helpful to know who has copies of a record, it is not necessary for each staff member to keep a copy of every piece of information if that information is available elsewhere in the corporate memory system.

The Principles of an Integrated Digital Environment

1. The owner/creator of information/data is the keeper and is responsible for its accuracy and timeliness.
2. Access to information replaces reporting.
3. Corporate memory (the essential evidence of an organization) is retained and is accessible in the "Knowledge Store" for reuse.

These principles can be articulated and arranged in various ways, but they accurately describe the integrated digital environment in which knowledge work can best be done. Reporting requirements can be reduced or eliminated as the same or better information is accessible once work is done in a web based environment. This single step creates immediate incentives to move to the web-based environment because it reduces some of the most onerous work of an organization.

Megill, Thinking for a Living. p. 98.

The best principle to follow is that the owner/creator is the keeper of information and others access that information by "looking over the shoulder" of the owner/creator.

In the modern organization, partly because of technology, information travels at a much faster speed and – even more importantly – takes many routes through an organization. A draft can be easily copied and forwarded electronically. Indeed, it is often the case that a draft is never finished. The recommendations of a report or a set of ideas may be implemented without a final report ever being issued because the draft has already been circulated about the organization. These drafts need to be saved because they are a part of the corporate memory since actions took place as a result of the information. Other drafts, however, where there is a final report, need not be saved.

Wordprocessing brought a revolution in the way in which information is managed in a corporate setting. More and more work is done by drafts that are circulated electronically and even implemented before they are approved and signed off. Wordprocessing software makes it easy to create multiple versions of a document, and a corporate memory management system can be made to distinguish between important and unimportant drafts and versions: obviously there is no reason to keep the original draft of a document after the spell checker is run. Also, minor changes made by the author need not be traced.

The rapid development of instant messaging, chat rooms, Listservs and other collaborative tools require procedures to be developed to determine what, if any, of the information products made in these environments need to be captured and made a part of the corporate memory. One good principle to follow is that if a committee or project team has met and discussed a document and a new version results, then keeping both versions for later use may be beneficial. The retention period for one version may be longer than another, but being able to keep multiple drafts or versions of a document is often important for understanding how a decision was made. On the other hand, except in the most sensitive situations there is little need to make a new version every time a document is changed. Identifying which drafts are more important than others should be a feature of a corporate memory management system. For now, let us simply note that not every draft needs to be kept.

Some copies of published materials

The publications of an organization are clearly part of the corporate memory. Publishing, by definition, means that information is made available and distributed to multiple users for multiple purposes. Published material is normally information that not everyone needs to have personal possession of at all times. Publishing enables material to be put into collections that are accessible by many users. Material is normally published so that information is available to persons outside the organization producing it. Materials published by other organizations are often useful, or potentially useful, to the organization and should be a part of the corporate memory. Maintaining potentially useful information from outside the organization is an important role traditionally played by the specialized library.

A library, one form of a knowledge store, is the repository of some corporate memory – normally the external information that is collected and kept for use by the members of the organization. Besides organizing and storing materials, a library is a source of information about where to find other information that may be needed. Special librarians realize that knowing where to find information is often more important than collecting all possibly relevant information. As the digital library expands, the need for individual organizations to maintain separate collections of published materials diminishes, whereas the need to know how and where to find what may be needed will increase.

Quotations and excerpts of published materials can be an important part of the corporate memory. Selections of published materials that are relevant to the business and notations of how to find useful publications are necessary parts of the corporate memory. In addition, there is value in keeping information on search strategies and methods adopted by others in the organization as a part of the corporate memory. Maintaining and categorizing these search strategies or scripts will be an important part of the work of the corporate memory manager. The identification of which information items belong to the corporate memory and which do not requires a combination of automated systems and information managers who can exercise judgment. Some items clearly belong to the corporate memory and others do not. Much of the information used in the organization lies somewhere in between. The cost of storage and retrieval will continue to be the driving factor in determining the quantity of material to become a part of the corporate memory. To distinguish between what needs to become a part of the corporate memory and what does not, we need to investigate and clarify the criteria to be used in valuing information. Applying these criteria in particular situations will enable a corporate memory system to be developed that meets the business needs of the organization.

CHAPTER FOUR

The document as a verb[7]

The corporate memory consists mainly of documents.[8] ISO standard 15489 defines a document (noun) as "recorded information or object which can be treated as a unit." This definition is a good one when we look at a document as an object – a noun.

However, in the Knowledge Age, a document is more often a verb than a noun. Knowledge is justified true belief.

We document our justifications (our reasons or evidence) for our beliefs so others may know the basis for our knowledge claim. Without documentation, we only have opinions. Gathering, preserving and presenting the evidence we have to justify our belief that something is true is an important part of preserving corporate memory. Traditionally, a document is a piece of paper or a collection of pieces of paper, which are

---

[7] This chapter was written with Leonard Mignerey, now the Vice-President of Product Engineering at Open-c Solutions located in Minneapolis, Minnesota. At the time we worked together on this chapter, he was the Director of Administrative Computing of Rutgers University. The discussion emerged out of an informal seminar conducted by the author and Mr. Mignerey at The Catholic University of America in 1995. We wish to thank all of the participants in that seminar for their contribution.

[8] "Documents are containers of information . . . A document is a human creation. It is created for a particular purpose and may be used for many other purposes. When a document is destroyed or lost the information it contains may no longer be available." Megill, Kenneth A. and Schantz, Herbert F., Document Management: New Technologies for the Information Services Manager. Munich: Saur . . . 1999.

Knowledge = Justified True Belief

Knowledge is a good and elevated word. Philosophers have chewed on it for centuries and have, at least in the Western philosophical tradition, come to the conclusion that it is "justified true belief." Philosophers, more than any other folks, worry about knowledge – what it is and how to acquire it. They call that discipline epistemology – the theory of knowledge."

Megill, Thinking for a Living, p. 73.

---

kept together because they were printed together. The document is generally bound or stapled. In a file folder there may be a number of documents put together, but each one is a discrete entity. On a library shelf a document is a discrete item, one that can be held and taken away. It can be charged out and returned.

The traditional document is an item because an author or a department or a producer decided that the items in the document had a common informational content and belonged together. The act of publishing or copying the document and distributing it identified it as an item that had meaning.

In the electronic age, 'document' is becoming a verb. Although traditional documents will continue to be used in some areas, as information moves to the electronic medium they are no longer items that need to be held, charged out and returned. In the digital world, documents need not be collected together physically. A link to a repository, normally held by the owner/creator, is sufficient and has the advantage of making the best available (normally the latest) version accessible. A document is the response to a query. It still means something, but the meaning is often determined not by the producer of the information, but by the questioner. Information that meant one thing to the producer can mean something very different when the elements of that document appear in answer to a query – and may mean something very different in answer to a different query.

The questioner

The electronic environment transforms information from being a static object that is owned by the producer and makes it valuable as a response to a question. A questioner can define the meaning of information, and knowing what questions to ask becomes a valuable skill. Traditional organizations are not designed for questioners. Indeed, loyalty and obedience are often the primary values in the traditional organization. However, loyalty, though important, often stifles creativity. Loyalty should be to a process that is open and expanding, not to a particular organizational structure. Disagreement is not disrespect.

The ability to formulate a question is at the core of humanity. A child wonders why something is the way it is and not another way. A child has imagination and can see connections that any reasonable adult knows are not there. A child can play. Indeed, the difference between play and work is often difference between questioning and following directions.

In the traditional organization, leisure is the absence of work: we are at leisure when we get off work. Working is following directions; we are creative in our leisure time. However, in the electronic environment the skills and activities traditionally associated with leisure time become paramount: we need to be able to relate to our fellow human beings; we need to be able to experiment; we need to play.

In a paper-based system it is fairly easy to decide what a document is: it consists of words on a sheet of paper and is generally the lowest level of organization for access to information.[9] A set of documents may be kept in a file folder. A document may be published. It is held together by a common meaning and use, and it is physically kept in one place.

In the electronic world, a document is often a compound of various files: it is no longer simply text on a sheet of paper. A document may be in a wordprocessing file that has an embedded reference to a spreadsheet. The spreadsheet is in a separate file that may be changed independently of the wordprocessed document. Whenever the wordprocessed document is called up, the current version of the spreadsheet appears and is put in its proper place. There may also be image files that are part of the document and maintained in other files. In other words, the document itself is not stored in a single place but is constructed each time it is needed.

---

[9] "The term document is narrower in scope than records; in paper-based record-keeping systems document usually means the ‚smallest unit of filing'; generally a single letter, form, report or other item housed in a filing system. This book is subtitled Document-Based Information Systems because the management of business documents is what information and records management, a professional management discipline, is all about. "Roebuck, Mary F., Brown, Gerald F. And Stephens, David O. Information and Records Management: Document-Based Information Systems. New York: Glencoe/McGraw-Hill, 1995. This definition is appropriate for a paper-based system, it does not hold when information is stored in electronic form.

Similarly, in relational databases data are maintained in many tables that can be accessed when needed. There is no single record kept. A document is created when needed from data stored in various tables. A student transcript, for example, is collected from data in a number of tables relating to the student (name, address, and social security number), courses taught at the university (course numbers, titles) and grades (including the term in which the grade was given). The transcript exists only when it is produced in response to a request. There is no place in the information system where the student's transcript is kept in the form in which it is to be displayed.

Documents, then, are becoming an answer to a query – a response given at a particular time and place. The query is made against a set of data which are updated from time to time. Document management is about workflow – not about managing objects. Managing documents is more about improving work processes than it is about collecting, organizing and arranging objects in a collection.

Beyond storage and retrieval

This new type of document dramatically changes the requirements for managing corporate information. Instead of just looking at how documents are created and the context in which they are found, we need to look at the function they perform and how they are used. The primary function of the information manager is no longer the storage and retrieval of physical documents. The corporate memory manager should be a part of an enterprise technical team with a particular responsibility for developing ways to document the activities of the business or organization.

Technology changes how organizations do business. In the precomputer age the function of document management was to bring physical records under control: to identify, store and retrieve the evidence of business transactions. Wordprocessing, relational databases imaging systems, electronic mail, instant messaging, and collaborative tools are profoundly changing the role of the corporate memory manager from one of storing to one of managing.

A document is a collection of related information, held together by a set of meanings that come from the author (and the intention of the author) and the user (and the perception of the user). A document may be in any medium or group of media, e.g. paper, electronic, photograph, microfilm. The value of a record is in its informational use as evidence. Once that use is gone, the value of the record is gone. If the evidence can be better found established in another medium or another place, then the prior record loses its value as the best available evidence.

In an organization, a record is an incarnation of an event or fact. It is an attempt to document (re-present) a process that is meaningful to the organization. It is a recording of a transaction or a group of related transactions.

Because of the historical technological limitations placed on the documentation process, we have a predisposition to think of documentation as a set of statically related facts fixed on a permanent medium. Traditionally this medium has been paper or film. We think of a record as a fixed object that can be identified, stored and retrieved. A record of this type can at best only document the processes of an enterprise in a sporadic and limited manner. Because a document is in a fixed form, the interval between documentation points is normally very great because only a few records are kept.

The technology that produces the new electronic document enables us to retrieve information at multiple points, depending upon our needs – not just when the information is preserved. The static bonds in which information is stored are broken and a process of dynamic information retrieval is unleashed.

Assembling a document

As a result of the development of new technologies, information is increasingly being stored as atomic entities, rather than as documents. An atomic entity cannot be further reduced without losing semantic content. In other words, it is the smallest unit of information that makes sense or has meaning. A document is assembled from time-stamped atomic entities in response to a query. Documents are collections of related information brought together through or for use.

We are not bound by what is contained in a particular document created at a particular time. We can access the stream of information as appropriate for each information request. If necessary, certain atomic entities can be documented as a continuous stream of information rather than as static snapshots in time. The pieces of information selected to construct a document are not limited to the same set of information gathered in the collection process. A request for a documented view, within a particular time context, may include atomic entities collected from different collection environments at different times.

Information belongs to the enterprise, not to the department. Duplicating enterprise information across multiple departments is wasteful and an impediment to information retrieval. Relational database technology makes it possible to view information from the enterprise level, rather than from the departmental level. The storage of information moves from the discrete-set-of-facts-per-record level to the atomic level. The standard report is no longer the only window into the information stream. Since information is stored as atomic entities, there are almost an infinite number of possibilities for information retrieval. Retrieval is no longer necessarily related to the way in which the information was collected and stored.

The documented view does not have to be archived as a physical object: it can be recreated on demand from the information stream. As time alters the value of specific documented views, subsequent recreations can expand, contract or duplicate previous documented views. For example, an initial business decision may be based on the contents of a particular document retrieved in response to several queries at a particular point in time. Later, if the decision is called into question, different questions can be posed against a very different data stream than was available when the initial decision was made. A new record can be dynamically constructed containing additional information relative to the context and contents of the original document.

To know where an electronic document is, we need to know where we stored the elements that make up that document. To do this it is helpful to know what the various versions of the document are, how they are stored and who has copies. Sometimes we may need to trace the use of documents in order to know who used what information when. All of these functions can be carried out by a robust corporate memory system.

The disintegration of centralized computing

In the past a file, a record or a publication consisted of one or more physical items (documents) assembled to meet the needs of a user. When computers first became major business tools, documents continued to be centrally managed and controlled. Data bases and other software managed the creation and assembly of documents, which could be virtual or physical documents. Now, however, the management and assembly process is done electronically for a user accessing data scattered throughout many information systems. Electronic storage enables the document to contain entities that are text, audio, video, graphic and static visual, all of which can be retrieved and associated dynamically.

As technology changes how data are stored, the value of the information that can be retrieved is increased and entirely new types and combinations of information become possible. Information products become a stream of atomic entities that support the information requirements of the enterprise, rather than a collection of documents held and managed centrally.

The disintegration of the document and the file is being accompanied by the disintegration of centralized computing. Networks bring the disintegration of physical storage of information to the next logical step. Networks scatter atomic entities and enable the user to reassociate them on demand. The user interface can sit on a desk in a department, in somebody's home, or on somebody's laptop. Information products (documents) can be called for and assembled by a myriad of computers – and even from machines that do not appear to be computers at all.

Business rules, which define how operations are carried out in a particular business, may exist in a business rule server that is located in corporate headquarters across the country. Information may be stored in multiple information servers, some local, some remote.

Local area networks (LANs) and their desktop personal computers provide a friendlier environment in which to use many applications. Computing power is moved from the center to the periphery, which opens up new opportunities for information management.

The business rules – the practices and procedures used by business – that were once 'owned' by various departments and work groups are now viewed from the perspective of the enterprise, rather than that of the department. Business rules are no longer linked to a particular application but can be applied throughout the organization. The result is to enable many user interfaces to access many business rules and many information entities. As the number of possible combinations expands, so does the potential for information usage. The static link between information collection and storage and information retrieval is broken forever.

The disintegration process has opened dramatic new ways for staff members to communicate. Hierarchical systems of control snap. Middle managers, whose primary function in the organization was to broker information, are replaced by a myriad of connections. As networks become connect to the networks, the individual workers literally has the whole world in the desktop – a world of information once accessible only to a privileged few.

Implications for the corporate memory

The development of the new type of document has profound implications for the development of the corporate memory system. Each of the information professions – librarianship, archive management and records management – based its work on managing physical documents. The librarian focused on published documents or technical reports, the archivist on items of historical significance, and the records manager on documents in a paper file. The disintegration of the documents as a physical object requires new ways for these professions to do their business.

The memory of an organization was once maintained primarily in discrete documents that could be identified, indexed, stored and retrieved – at least in principle. With the new type of document the possibilities of capturing the memory of an institution are greatly increased. We can know more than those who were in the situation, not just because we have the advantage of hindsight but because our information systems enable us to ask and answer questions that were not possible earlier.

The emergence of the new document means that we need to re-examine the traditional ways in which we manage records and documents. Although technology will help us in this endeavor, the solution to management problems will not be found merely by applying technology. It is in rethinking and re-engineering our work that we begin to develop the tools and techniques appropriate for documents and records management in the electronic age. The challenge becomes how to document transactions. Document becomes a verb – the process of determining which questions to ask to ensure that the corporate memory is properly documented. The new document requires new procedures and new kinds of information managers to document the corporate memory.

CHAPTER FIVE

Valuing documents

We turn now to the task of managing the new documents – the verbs that make up our business life as our work increasingly focuses on answering knowledge questions – "Is it a good idea to . . .?"

Some, but not all, information is worth keeping for re-use and is therefore part of the corporate memory. We need to determine what to keep and what not, and how long to keep those items we do decide to keep. In traditional records management calculations, less than two per cent of the records of an organization are worthy of permanent retention, i.e. housing in a permanent archive. More are worth keeping for a limited time. A number of the records created in an electronic environment are of transitory value and need not be kept for reuse. They are not part of the corporate memory, even though they may be evidence of transactions that need to be kept for a period of time.

In Chapter 3 we discussed many information products (also called information packets) that are not created by or used by an organization that are not part of corporate memory. These include purely personal information, copies of information that is kept elsewhere, and some drafts and versions of documents.

Not keeping this information and identifying how information kept elsewhere can be retrieved when needed in its most reliable version is the first (and sometimes the hardest) step in managing the corporate memory.

Once the determination is made that a packet or product of information is worth keeping for re-use, the process of valuing that information can begin – for not all information that should be kept for re-use has the same value and the value of information changes over time and is different for different users.

Some information is more valuable than others, and determining the value of a document is one of the most important and difficult tasks. The worst approach to the problem is to ignore it. In this chapter we shall develop a number of rules of worth that can be used by an organization to determine the value of information. These rules can also be used to design automated systems to manage corporate memory.

In using these rules, we need to bear in mind some of the characteristics of information:

* Most information is of value for a finite period.
* As the business needs of an organization change, the length of time records should be kept changes.
* There should be a specific time for keeping each type of record that is worth keeping.
* The value of information often depends on the existence of other information.
* Information often gains value in context.
* As information is linked to other information, the length of time it should be kept will change.
* Information may be valuable because someone else finds a use for it.
* Information ages over time. Sometimes it increases in value, like a good carpet or fine wine, but most often information loses value as it ages.
* Some information can simply be replaced when it is updated.
* In order for information to be of value, it must be of use to someone for some purpose.
* Information has value in relation to its use or possible reuse.

Corporate information needs to be managed because it is or may be of value to someone other than the person or group who created it. The determination of how long to keep information concerns not just the viewpoint of the person or group creating it but that of the organization as a whole.

Confidentiality and privacy

Of course, some information is private and does not belong in the corporate memory at all. Other information is confidential and belongs in the corporate memory, but access may need to be restricted. Since the purpose of a corporate memory system is to make information available for reuse, restrictions on access should be minimized and inappropriate information should not be stored. All information should have a retention date applied to it when it is created. If there is restricted access to information (if it is confidential to some degree), the restrictions should also be given a particular time limit.

The determination of what is private, confidential or restricted is an important part of valuing information. As a basic principle, all information created in the process of doing business belongs in the corporate memory. Restrictions to access should be limited, since the information in the corporate memory belongs to the corporation and may have unexpected value to others. In practice, however, much information is not valuable for reuse. By limiting the corporate memory to those items that may be reused, some of the problems of confidentiality and privacy can be avoided.

The Question of Worth

The technology that creates the conditions leading to information loss also gives us the tools necessary to develop systems to manage the corporate memory. The medium on which the information is stored (paper, hard-drive of a personal computer, a server, microfiche etc.) should not determine how long it is kept, nor should that decision be based on its source (generated internally within the organization or received from outside). The decision on how long to keep information should be based on its content – its meaning – and the possibility of its future reuse.

The question of worth or value is at the heart of developing a corporate memory management system. The tools and techniques developed by records and archive management to determine how long to keep record can help us determine the value of information. Records managers have traditionally used file plans and a retention (or disposition) schedule: a retention schedule categorizes all records in an organization and tells staff what to keep, how long to keep it and in what format. Ideally, a retention schedule should identify every possible packet of information created by an organization, how long it should be kept and in what format. An inventory of all record types is the starting point for traditional records management. In practical terms, however, a complete inventory is seldom possible. The value of any given record changes as the activities of the organization change. In addition, the length of time a record is kept depends on other records or events that cannot be determined in advance. As we shall see later in Chapter Nine when we discuss workflow, registering a document is an important step in determining its value and place with context of the information of an organization.

Case files

Most, but not all, files are "case" files. A "case" file opens and closes – it documents an activity with a beginning and an end.[10] A set of documents relating to a project could be kept for 5 years after the project has ended. In this case, all relevant files need to be linked to that project. In most organizations a majority of information is kept in what records managers call case files, which begin and end at a specific time. They may be personnel files that are opened when a person is hired (or interviewed) and closed when the person leaves the organization. They may be vendor files that open when a vendor is first used and closed when the vendor goes out of business or has not been used for a particular period. In a law firm, a case file refers to a particular matter handled by the firm. In an architectural firm it may be a particular project. Eighty-five percent of the textual records in federal agencies are arranged by case, according to the manual on case filing distributed by the National Archives and Records Administration.

Most case files need to be kept for a certain number of years after the case is closed or the project is finished. For example, an employee's file closes when the employee leaves the organization, but it is unlikely that the file needs to be kept permanently. A particular piece of information needs to be organized according to the case to which it is relevant. The value of the information will be determined largely by the importance of the case to the organization, not by the importance of the particular piece of information.

Of course, one reason to have a corporate memory system is to be able to use information generated for one case or project in another. Much of the work of an organization consists of similar activities, and information is valuable for reuse if it can be taken from one case file and modified for use in a similar activity.

---

[10] A case file can be contrasted with a subject file, which generally has no particular beginning or end. Good records management practice calls for subject files to be cut-off (closed) annually or at some other regular interval.

Box 5.1 Cut off your files before they cut you off

As a poster of the National Archives and Records Administration puts it, you need to 'cut off your files before they cut you off'. The poster shows a man surrounded by filing cabinets and cut off from the outside world. He is, vainly, trying to climb over them, without much success.

The National Archives, like most organizations charged with managing paper records, argues that files must be cut off at regular intervals so they can be properly managed. Cutting off files is particularly difficult when they contain subjects, or items within the same subject, that have differing values. A records manager who subscribes to the importance of cutting off files often urges offices to start their subject files over again each year. Such a system can work, but it is an unusual office that agrees to manage all of its information by starting new subject files each year.

As records are generated and kept in electronic form, information is no longer physically stored by subject and the advice to cut off files regularly becomes irrelevant.

Case files are closed when the case is over or finished. For routine business activities, the closing of a case file is triggered by an external event, but as most records managers know, getting a case file closed is sometimes difficult because it is not always easy to determine when something is really over.

A case file normally has a number of documents "in" it. The identification of the kinds of documents (information packets) is an important part of the file plan.

In an electronic environment the information in a case file will be scattered throughout the organization's information base. Proper indexing, and showing how one set of information is linked to others, is necessary so that information can be retrieved. Items in files will not normally be stored together and the information may be of value to a number of different cases.

In paper systems, a user was often handed a case file and was responsible for finding the appropriate item within the file. With automated document management systems, documents can be retrieved without getting the whole case file. The case file continues to play a function in an automated system, even if the user never sees the case file as a physical object. The case file provides the "provenance" – the context in which the information is collected and, as any archivist or records manager knows, often the best way to find information needed is by looking through a file for similar documents that are "near" a document of interest.

A document may be located "in" more than one case file. In a paper system this was accomplished by making copies and putting a copy in every relevant file. In an automated system, these links to where else a document may be "located" can add significantly to information about a document and make it more useful.

With properly registered documents, however, physical copies need not be made, but one of the important bits of information (metadata) about a document is which case file it belongs in – and what else is in that case file.

Subject files

Subject files are traditionally kept together because they are about the same subject. They are normally arranged in alphabetical order with information about the same topic filed together. The problem is that most information packets are about more than one thing. In most offices, handling paper subject files causes great difficulty. Often subjects are not clearly defined – or cannot be clearly defined – in advance. Managing a subject file in a manual system is difficult and most do not have a cut-off date. Since they are not closed on a routine basis, the only way to remove outdated material is to go through the files. Records managers know that, despite the best intentions, almost no-one ever takes the time to do this. Instead, files normally age, sometimes gracefully and sometimes not, until they are either forgotten or destroyed. Records managers urge the development of filing systems in which all subject files are cut off each year.

Automation provides another way to approach the problem of subject files. A subject file is created to make access to information possible. Unfortunately, in a manual system there is only one access point in a subject file. Sometimes a document may be copied and put in two or three places to provide more access points. To retrieve information, it is necessary to remember how it was filed. In other words, the thought processes of the person who filed the document must be recreated, something that is often very difficult years later.

A subject file can be a powerful tool, for it brings information together in the same place and enables us to make unexpected associations. In an automated system, many subjects can be assigned to each document. In addition, a controlled vocabulary (often developed in a logically related way and called a thesaurus) can be developed to make sure that the subject terms are used consistently. In other words, if 'personnel' means 'human relations', then 'human relations' is substituted whenever the term 'personnel' is chosen by a staff member. The development of a thesaurus of terms for an organization is often one of the most important contributions of the information professional.

In an automated system, information does not need to be stored physically by subject in order to be easily retrieved. An adequate corporate memory system needs to have the capability for browsing as well as retrieving particular items. The use of multiple subject terms to describe what information is about significantly increases access to information. When subject is combined with other terms (such as author, date, office of origin etc.) the ability to retrieve information expands greatly.

The significant increase in access to information is made possible through the use of meta-data, data "about" the document. In the registration process, meta-data that includes both the case files in which it belongs as well as the relevant subjects that pertain to the document. Metadata need not be static and can (and should) be added to or altered as needed and appropriate. In an automated environment, the corporate memory manager does his or her job primarily through the management of meta-data. One of the most important pieces of metadata – and what makes a corporate memory system – is the addition of retention guidelines for every document and every information element.

Retention schedules

In order for a corporate memory system to operate effectively, definite retention schedules are needed for all information no matter what kind of files they are in. It is of no value, for example, to say that information should be kept until not needed or as long as necessary. A good corporate management system enables the corporate memory manager to review classes of information, or even items that are scheduled for destruction and, if necessary, change the retention period. A properly constructed schedule does not eliminate the need for judgments to be made but allows them to be made both prior to and at the time of record creation.

Throughout the process of determining the value of information, it is important that the four traditional tests be used as a guide:

- Functional needs: what information is needed to do business?
- Administrative needs: what information is needed for administrative purposes?
- Legal requirements: what information must be kept by law?
- Historical needs: what information should be kept permanently?

Keeping too much is often as harmful to the corporate memory as keeping too little, and so it is essential that every document has a fixed period given to it at the time of creation. The retention schedule may change as the needs of the organization change, or if the information becomes valuable in unexpected ways or it becomes linked with other documents with a longer retention. But there should be no retentions such as "until no longer needed" or "until superceded".

Rules as guidelines

The rules formulated here are guidelines to be used when exercising judgment. They were developed in the practice of professional archivists and records managers examining documents to decide their value. In an automated corporate memory management system these guidelines need to become an important part of automated procedures, while enabling judgment to supersede the strict application of rules.

Worth is a qualitative, not a quantitative, evaluation. Each of these rules formulates principles that see the value of information to be in a continuum and dependent on many factors. We can, however, make determinations that establish routines to manage the corporate memory without having an army of information professionals making judgments on the value of each individual item or allowing the creator of a document to determine it value.

Rule of Worth I: Information used by important people is more likely to be important information

Important people in an organization may be at any level in the hierarchy. They are often the staff members closest to the delivery of goods or services. In a modern organization they also include top management. Often, the information that arrives to upper management is sanitized and only partially documents the decision-making procedure. To obtain all the information that should be kept in the corporate memory, a determination of both formal and informal important people needs to be made.

The information closest to the delivery of goods and services is often seen as being at the bottom of the organization, and it should be the basis for all decisions made in the organization. As you move up the ladder, information is aggregated and interpreted. The middle level of management adopts a tactical point of view and adds value to the information, creating summaries based on records of the transactions. The aggregation of information is an important activity of management.

The responsibility of the leaders of an organization is to provide the strategic leadership and vision. Traditionally, for the records manager, and to a lesser extent for the archivist, the value of information is determined by how high up the organizational structure the information is used. For example, nearly everything created or used by the Board of Directors is presumed to be important. So, too, is information associated with the office of the president, and with those who report directly to this office. As one moves down the organizational hierarchy, the importance of the information is presumed to diminish.

This model works in a paper-based office: a memo moves through the chain and is signed off at each stage in the chain. A draft is clearly a draft, and is not normally seen by the next level above in the chain until it is finished – approved and signed off by the level below.

In the age of teams and less hierarchical management, such systems may no longer identify the important persons in an organization. Electronic information flows in many directions and the distinction between operations and management blurs. Often this phenomenon is seen in the demise of the middle manager, but it is really an indication that technology enables those closest to the operation to make decisions once reserved for management. The important people may now be at any level of the organization.

It is still possible to determine who is important in an organization. Once this is done, information used by and sent to these people can normally be considered a part of the corporate memory. Some of this information will need to be restricted to certain individuals for a time, a task that can be handled by an adequate corporate memory system. The principle that the value of information is determined, at least partially, by the position of the office using or producing it still holds. In designing the corporate memory system we need to capture most of the material in the most important offices in the system. We also need to develop systems that identify as the most important version or draft of a document the one used by the most important persons in an office. Much of this can be automated using available technology.

Rule of Worth II: Information takes on value when it is used

Document creators are often the least appropriate people to determine the retention period for the information they create. Creators can determine the type of document and how it fits into the file plan, but the decision about retention is a business decision, not a personal decision. The author cannot have the perspective needed and may have interests that are contrary to the corporate interest in retaining information that is of value for re-use.

Information is of value only if it is useful. One indication that information is useful is that it is shared. Such information is more likely to be a candidate for reuse, and therefore to be a part of the corporate memory. In designing the corporate memory system, therefore, we need to identify when an item of information is shared and to decide at that point if it should enter the corporate memory. A version worth identifying as a new version is normally one sent to someone else to read or review. The corporate memory management system needs to capture documents at the point when they are shared with another person or unit.[11]

Dissemination of information is seen from at least two perspectives – that of the person sending out the information and that of the person receiving it. Some information may also be of value to other parties: for example, it may aid the organization in presenting its programs and enhancing its image for the public. Other information may have a historical or social value that extends beyond the persons involved in producing and sharing it.

By analyzing who uses information and how widely it is used, we can determine the use of information both within and outside an organization. By studying use patterns we can obtain some indicators of the value of the information. Information that is widely disseminated and used should be made a part of the corporate memory.

There may be some counter examples to this rule, such as important information that is a trade secret or highly restricted. Normally such information would be captured in the corporate memory under the previous rule that information used by important people is likely to have value.

Rule of Worth III: Vital records are a part of the corporate memory

Records managers have long identified a vital records program as an important part of records management. Vital records are those that are necessary for the business to operate. A vital records program is a part of a disaster-preparedness program, which every business should have in order to recover information in case of a fire, earthquake or other

---

[11] Some routine information that is widely disseminated (appeals to contribute to charity, announcements of social events and other activities of interest to the entire organization) may have only a very short retention period. These announcements may, however, provide a good indication of the life of the organization.

disaster. In developing the corporate memory management system, items that are essential to keep the business operating need to be identified and should be stored in an alternative location and refreshed at regular intervals. If information is vital for a company to function, it is by definition a part of the corporate memory.

Rule of Worth IV: Historical information is valuable

One reason for keeping information is for its historical value. Historical information is important for the development and preservation of the corporate culture. By understanding the organization's origins, it is possible to know why decisions are made in the way they are. Sometimes historical information can be valuable in enabling the organization to identify trends and to understand what products or ways of doing business have become fashionable and then passed away. The identification of historical trends can assist the organization in its decision-making. The historical nature of records is particularly important for government. In many countries, including the United States, the control of government records rests with the archivist, who is charged with making sure that historically important records are kept.

In practice, the historian is often reduced to dealing with whatever records are available. If your interest is in fourteenth century Irish art, the sources you have to work with may be so scarce that every remaining piece of evidence is of historical value. On the other hand, if you are working on World War II there may be a surfeit of documents. Then, the historian can choose from the available documents what may be of value for a particular project. A historian looks at information from a long-term perspective and from the perspective of society as a whole, rather than that of a single institution.

The determination of what is of historical value should be made in consultation with a historian, who will be interested primarily in records that will be kept permanently and transferred to an archive. There are some packets of information that will be of great interest to the historian but of little interest to the corporation. These include samples of records that reflect the culture of the institution at a particular time. For this reason, the theory of sampling developed within the archival profession can be of particular value in selecting information to keep for purely historical purposes.[12]

---

[12] The manuals of the Society of the American Archivists provide the guidelines to make decisions of historical value.

In an electronic environment the historically valuable information records can be determined at the time of creation and transferred to the archives. An archive can thus be an important repository of information, which can develop to serve the ongoing business needs of an organization.

Of course the appropriate records for an organization will vary, but the following are normally historically important documents:

- minutes of Board meetings;
- corporate records, such as articles of incorporation;
- annual reports;
- all publications;
- organizational charts;
- memoranda of long-term agreements with other organizations.

Rule of Worth V: Information whose retention is required by law or regulation is valuable for the period specified in the law or regulation

Just as historians are the proper persons to decide what information is historically valuable, so the general counsel is the appropriate official to decide what should be kept for legal purposes and for how long it should be kept. It is important, from a legal perspective, that information be kept as long as necessary but no longer.

One result of managing the corporate memory will be to establish a system that enables an organization to purge its information system regularly to avoid keeping unnecessary information. If an organization has an approved information management system developed in accordance with the law, then destruction of information is permitted.

Most organizations run into difficulties because they keep multiple sets of documents and information. If there is a legal case, then these are candidates for discovery. Unmanaged records and information systems are potential time-bombs waiting to explode. Much of the justification for a system to manage corporate memory can come from legal authority.

To decide exactly what is the required time to keep documents, the corporate memory manager should be familiar with the codes and norms of the business. Often trade associations or professional organizations provide guidelines for the retention of records, which will vary depending upon the jurisdiction in which the organization is located. When an organization is in multiple jurisdictions, then it is important that all relevant rules and regulations be followed.

Applying the Rules of Worth

Let us take an example of applying the rules of worth to the records of the office of a government agency charged with chartering new financial institutions. These records might include:

- Charter application;
- staff actions relating to application;
- hearing records, including testimony, exhibits, decision etc.;
- recommendations and internal staff deliberations;
- record of decision-making body;
- e-mail messages relating to particular decisions
- telephone logs or notes;
- notes of discussions;
- wordprocessed documents;
- record of final determination.

Each of these record types needs to be examined in terms of value. Some may be of historical value and may need to be kept permanently, for example the record of an official action adopted by the Board or chief executive.

The initial application, once the decision has been made, may need to be kept for a few weeks in the office processing the application. It might be useful for a longer period of time as an example or a precedent. For administrative purposes, it might be necessary to keep it for several years, in case there is a question about how the decision was made (administrative purposes). There might be a legal requirement to keep the application for a specific period of time, and the legal department might want the record kept for a few years, in case fraudulent statements were made on the application. The historian, however, might want to keep the application as a part of the permanent record, for it would be an excellent source to learn the history of a community – who was in a position to apply for a new financial institution, what relationships existed, etc.

As time goes on, requirements may change, so it is important to document why a decision is made to keep a document, when it is made, as well as why it was decided to make one record permanent and to keep another for a short period of time. As circumstances change, then the length of time that documents are kept can be changed as well.

A good system to manage corporate memory must be able to cope with change. An organization may be merged with another, or thoroughly reorganize itself. A project that once seemed unimportant may later turn out to be very important, and therefore more valuable. The value of information is determined largely by its use; it is not static: when its use changes, its value changes. The development of a system to determine the retention of information is an important part of developing a corporate memory system.

When different rules yield differing results (for example when the historian and the attorney disagree on how long to keep information), the longer period should prevail. As information is valued – i.e. as retention decisions are made – the reasons for these decisions need to be kept as well. As conditions change, it will be possible to change the retention periods for groups of documents.

CHAPTER SIX

The corporate memory manager

The purpose of the corporate memory system is to bring the user as close to the information as possible. A system that yields an answer such as 'Go to x, y or z' is not sufficient. Pointers to information are not enough as more and more information is in electronic form. Information needs to be accessible directly, not just through catalogs or indexes. As we shall see later, advances in searching and browsing technologies enable information, and not just pointers to information, to be accessed.

This does not mean that cataloging and indexing activities will disappear. In fact, the need for marking and organizing information increases in an electronic environment, since searching and browsing systems rely on these markings in order to discover the information the user needs. Many of the activities of information intermediaries can be automated. In the end, however, there will be a continuing and expanding role for information professionals, to formulate and conduct searches and develop systems that promote effective browsing and searching.

Initially, most departments in charge of automation saw their role as supporting traditional business processes. Since most of the staff was skilled and trained in mainframe technology, they were far more accustomed to working with machines than with users. As the focus shifts from data to work processes, even short-term historical data spans generations of technology. As the length of time in which a particular generation of technology shortens, individuals are needed who understand what records and documents are and what they mean to an enterprise – not as static accumulations of facts, but as on-demand, dynamic views of the organization that can support long-term and short-term historical needs, daily needs, and the future needs of the organization.

For the foreseeable future corporate memory managers must face the almost impossible task of performing two very different jobs at the same time. In addition to planning and implementing technological initiatives that put organizations on the path to the virtual document of the future, they must apply current and emerging technology to traditional document/records management problems. This challenge is and will continue to be fraught with difficulty, because of the rate of technological change. Corporate memory managers will have to manage information projects across the boundaries of technological change – often across the boundaries of a number of technology generations. The corporate memory manager has skills found in several currently separate professions.

Like a records manager, the corporate memory manager needs to understand how to determine the value of records, how long they need to be kept and how they can best be stored. The records manager is also

---

Box 6.1 The corporate memory manager

Corporate memory managers are distinguished from other information managers because they cut across many traditional organizational and professional lines. Corporate memory managers may come from one or more of several different professions. When asked how they came to their present position, they normally say by accident.

The corporate memory manager is characterized by openness to innovation and change and to managing information regardless of its source. Internal and external information can be managed using the same tools and techniques. Internal and external customers often have the same needs.

The corporate memory manager focuses on the creation, control and dissemination of information in order to meet customer needs. The corporate memory manager is primarily a manager of information, one of the important resources of the organization. The corporate memory manager is therefore also an important part of the management of the organization.

The combination of skills – technical, business and managerial – is what characterizes the corporate memory manager. The willingness to look beyond current boundaries is a part of the daily activities of the corporate memory manager.

acutely aware of the problems that come with the migration of technologies, for information is often stored in media that are no longer accessible using the organization's current technology.

Like an archivist, the corporate memory manager needs to understand how to identify historically important information that may be of value to users with very different needs than those who generate and use information in the day-to-day operation of the business. The archivist is also schooled in the art of appraisal – determining the value of information, especially historical information, so that strategies can be found to preserve it. The corporate memory manager, like the archivist, is concerned with the adequacy of documentation and the necessity to create information that may or may not be generated in the normal activities of the organization.

Like librarians, the corporate memory manager understands the skills of text searching and finding information regardless of its location. He or she needs to know how to access and retrieve external information that may be needed by the organization.

Above all, the corporate memory manager must know the business of the organization and be able to apply the skills and techniques of the information disciplines to meet corporate or organizational needs. He or she needs to understand the capabilities of current storage media and how to work with technical teams to meet the memory needs of the organization. An awareness of the nature of the enterprise, its products and its services, is necessary.

Finally, the corporate memory manager needs to be able to identify information as a resource of the organization and to assess the value of the information generated by and used by the organization. Adding value to information by integrating it and making it available throughout the organization and as a product of the organization is the fundamental task of the corporate memory manager.

The focus of the corporate memory manager is at the enterprise level rather than the department level, although the goal of the work is to make information accessible at the department and project level where the work is done. The function will change from one that is generally reactive – 'What are we going to do with this accumulation of records?' – to one that is integral to the strategic planning process of the enterprise. The traditional custodial focus of the profession diminishes as the responsibility for the integrity of the record shifts to the automated system. Extensive systems analysis skills and business acumen are required for the information manager to succeed at this level of the organization.

Corporate memory managers will participate in the design of information architectures so that the correct pieces of atomic information can be assembled within the correct time intervals to support the processes and information needs of tomorrow's organizations. Like previous records managers, the records managers of the future will focus on developing procedures (business rules) to identify information that is important to the operation of the organization.

It is now widely recognized that document management is a part of information management rather than facilities management. The tools and techniques of information management can be applied to the management of documents. Records, from this point of view, are in-house collections of information. The same type of information access as is available through online services can be used to manage these collections of information. The corporate memory manager combines internal with external information. The corporate memory manager should be part of the technical team that determines how work is done, since he or she is responsible for one of the most important assets of the organization – its information. Like a good special librarian, a good corporate memory manager must be knowledgeable about the business of the organization while at the same time relating to the external information world. He or she needs to be able to integrate the information needs of programs that may operate with relatively little contact with other programs that use or produce similar information, bringing together the products of parts of the organization and make them available for the rest of the organization and beyond. The integration of information is one of the tasks of the corporate memory manager. As a practical matter, this activity may be carried out at many places within the organization: in the records department, the archives, the library, the office of information technology or even the office of the general counsel.

Managing the corporate memory requires more than just computing: it is an information task. If the organization has a chief information office, it should be assigned responsibility for the organization-wide management of the corporate memory. The corporate memory is one of the most valuable assets of the organization and should receive the same care and attention as other major assets such as cash, property and employees. If there is no person clearly responsible for maintaining the corporate memory of the organization, then those involved in various information activities need to take on that role as best they can.

The effective management of the corporate memory requires a staff with quite different skills than most information managers have today. At present, most of these managers are trained as technicians who focus on acquiring and installing technology, not on managing the content of information. The skills needed by corporate memory managers are found in various professions, such as information management, librarianship, archiving and records management. Other professionals, such as those in charge of management information systems, data management and information resources management, have some of the skills required to manage the corporate memory properly. Each of these professions can learn from the others. Whichever profession the corporate memory manager may come from, he or she will need to be familiar with all of them.

Each of these professions, under the force of rapid technological developments in its field, is undergoing profound and rapid change. Some believe that, over time, a single profession of information management may emerge. Others believe that the various professions will maintain their separate identities and will work together as a team in organizational settings.

The corporate memory manager needs to be a member of many work teams. Duties may include providing advice to management regarding workflow questions, working with lawyers to determine the appropriate disposition of information needed for legal purposes, and working as a member of project groups that have an information component. This last is becoming an increasingly important part of the information manager's job.

The focus of the corporate memory manager is on the content of the information needed by the organization to meet customer needs, not the form in which it is managed. Knowledge of technology and the ability to work with technicians is also important.

By definition, the management of corporate memory must be an integrative process. Document systems often fail to provide crucial information that cannot be captured merely by saving the document. Besides capturing information, knowledge is needed to determine what the document is about – what key activities or words describe the content of the information in the document that may or may not be found in the words in the document itself. In addition, we need to know who has received copies of the document, where else it is stored, and the various media in which it is stored. All of this information improves the ability to retrieve information from the corporate memory.

The records manager

The core business activities of the records manager are storing and retrieving records. The way in which records are organized is therefore of some interest. The primary job, however, is to take away and organize unwanted files in case someone needs them again.

The records manager was traditionally thought to be part of facilities management, rather than the information profession. Since the records manager was primarily involved with the management of file folders rather than the information contained within them, the management of records was rather like managing furniture. Now, most records managers see their jobs as managing information, not just the containers of information. A document, once seen as the lowest level of filing, is often a compound of elements stored in several locations. A records manager needs to understand the information flow of the organization and how documents can be identified and stored.

If a record is one particular kind of document, a records manager is one kind of document manager, managing documents that serve as evidence of business processes. A records manager is rooted in the business of the organization, and part of the overarching field of document management. Many records managers now call themselves 'records and information managers' and ARMA, the Association of Records Managers and Administrators, has decided to use only the initials ARMA with the tag line 'the organization of information professionals'.[13]

The records management profession places great emphasis on the concept of retention schedules (sometimes called disposition schedules). Every piece of paper should have a retention period attached to it, so that we know when and how it should be destroyed. The records manager took inactive records from departments and saved money by freeing up expensive office space. They transferred the records to off-site storage (or less expensive on-site storage) and, at the proper time, destroyed them according to the disposition schedule.

The initial automation of records management processes used the tools and techniques developed for warehouses and other storage facilities. Space management became the key for records management. Storing, fetching and reshelving were the primary activities. Moving and storage companies recognized that storing records was not much different from storing furniture, and applied their techniques to the world of records management. As a result, the automation of warehousing led to great increases in efficiencies in records management.

---

[13] This was the case when the first edition of this book was written. Since then, ARMA, like other organizations, has continued to search for its identity and for words to describe what its members do.

The application of barcode technology greatly accelerated the physical storage and retrieval of paper records. At first, barcode technology was used to keep track of boxes. Later, the same technology migrated down to folders. Vendors that had specialized in shelving and developing elaborate color coded filing systems discovered that adding bar-coding greatly increased the efficiency of filing room operations.

The initial application of bar-coding technology to records management did not change the way in which work was done, but it greatly increased the speed and accuracy of storing and retrieving records. Those who managed warehouses had long ago noticed that what was being managed was space, not items. Instead of seeing warehouses as being full of items, operators began to see them as spaces to be managed. When this concept was applied to records management and used with bar-coding technology, it was no longer necessary to store like things in the same place. With an automated tracking system, items could be put in any available space, allowing fuller utilization of the space in the records storage area.

Applying space management principles to the records business opens up dramatic new ways to save space and money. Previously, records managers, taking their lead from archivists, had assumed that like records had to be stored together, and so when similar records came into the warehouse they would be physically placed next to other records of the same kind. For example, records from Department Y were stored in a specific space reserved for Department Y.

The problem came, however, when records were recalled from storage. Sometimes records were checked out for months or even years, and the empty space had to be kept waiting for these records to be returned. Sometimes a large volume of records needed to be withdrawn for a considerable period of time. Sometimes when the records were returned there were more than had initially been set out, because new material had been added. This was particularly the case where extensive litigation was involved.

Records managers asked, 'Why not simply take incoming records, affix barcodes and store them in any available space?' When time came for the records to be retrieved – either for recall or for eventual destruction – the computer could generate a list of locations and the records could be removed. Records managers changed their focus from moving boxes to managing space, which naturally led to a focus on managing the flow of work. The same skills are useful in the digital environment.

Back in the file room, meanwhile, a similar revolution was going on. Why should paper copies of a document be kept if the document was in digital form? Could not a wordprocessed document replace the paper

---

Box 6.2 The contemporary records manager

The transformation of the records manager from a facilities manager to an information manager is well under way. The major association of records managers in the United States, the Association of Records Managers and Administrators (ARMA), recently changed its name to ARMA International and added a tag line, 'The Information Management Professionals'.

The reality of the work of the contemporary records manager is deeply tied up with the rapid proliferation of electronic records. The development of networked systems and, above all, e-mail, means that the records manager works closely with technology and developing technology.

The contemporary records manager must understand technology and where it is going. Equally importantly, the contemporary records manager must be able to manage records that exist in a variety of media, some of which are no longer used. For example, many records are still on microfilm, once one of the most popular media.

Records managers now call themselves records and information managers, or simply information managers. Often this is more than a name change, as records management functions migrate to those parts of the organization responsible for information management. The information manager becomes a part of technical teams to design systems that document the activities of the organization.

---

copy? The initial answer was a loud 'no'. Only the paper copies had the valid signatures and only the paper copies had the marginalia (notes). The record copy would always be the paper copy – or so it was thought.

The arrival of imaging technology and internet technology changed all that. Electronic image management systems enabled paper documents to be scanned at the point of entry into the business and then forwarded to where they were needed. The internet enabled documents or elements of documents to be stored and retrieved anywhere on a world-wide network. Initially the workflow remained the same. Images were collected into folders just as paper had been. Case files were created and document management of electronic images was just the same as for paper, but much faster, but the technologies for new ways to do work were there.

The transformation of records managers into information managers came with the convergence of image technology, wordprocessing and the arrival of networking. Thus, as more information was kept in electronic form and large central file rooms became obsolete, records managers shifted from being managers of warehouses to being managers of information.

As records managers became part of the information management team, copying of records in electronic form took on a greater role than fetching and checking out documents. Image technology provides the tool to automate document management. With the help of tools to manage wordprocessed documents in a networked environment, the records manager becomes an information manager.

Increasingly, the contemporary information manager continues to move away from the realm of facilities management and files management and increasingly plays an important part in managing the internal corporate memory of the organization.

Librarians

Librarians have always been concerned with information. Librarians collect, select, organize, shelve, charge out, charge in and weed collections of information. They learn where to find information on a particular subject and have developed techniques to describe what subject terms apply to a particular packet of information. In their traditional role, however, librarians often did not organize information – they collected and organized containers of information and put these containers together with others containers that had similar subjects. Librarians are particularly skilled at putting information together so that it can be browsed.

Classifying is the tool traditionally used to put like items together. The containers of information might be books or journals. Sometimes they are objects in special collections, such as photographs or music scores. These containers are organized according to various classification schemes, which often become more complicated as collections grow. Within the library profession specialized classifiers were needed to decide where the containers belong within a collection. These specialists were called catalogers.

Librarians developed a system that represents each document with a document surrogate consisting of specific descriptors, applied by classifiers and stored in a separate tagged field database standardized as the machine readable code (MARC) record. The complex rules for creating each descriptive element were standardized as the Anglo-American Cataloging Rules, 2nd edition (AACR2) and as subject heading lists created by national organizations, such as the Library of Congress and the National Library of Medicine.

Catalogers developed records – surrogates that point to information. These are often called bibliographic records, of which the traditional catalog card is the most familiar example. Surrogates do not contain the information, but are used to find the containers. These containers are then brought to the user, who finds and uses the appropriate information.

Librarians are skilled intermediaries. They know how to organize containers of information and how to help users find the proper container. Reference books proliferate that serve as aids to the librarian and, over time, a complex profession arose based on the management of surrogates.

Librarians worked on the assumption that containers are collected and then dispersed. Collection development was at the heart of the profession.

The transformation of the work of librarians away from collection management began with online searching. It accelerated as searching moved from being a specialized tasks requiring professional skill to an every-day activity of the end users equipped with automated browsing tools. Online technology enabled librarians to easily access collections not their own. Instead of collecting and organizing items, attention shifted to identifying where information can be found, regardless of its physical location.

Initially, accessing information online did not disrupt the traditional work of the librarian: it merely enabled certain kinds of reference work to be done faster. The initial online items were bibliographic entries, abstracts and index terms. They were generally electronic versions of abstracts and indexes that continued to be published and delivered on paper. Indeed, the companies who created and managed online databases were initially the same companies who managed and published the paper indexes. Paper companies owned the electronic access systems for online databases and inflated pricing to take into account the need to protect the existence of the paper-based indexes.

In time, the online industry was bought by publishing companies and the transformation of the way information was collected and dispersed took another step forward. In addition to publishing books, journals, magazines and newspapers (the traditional containers of information), publishing companies began to make the information packets themselves available on the world-wide network.

As time went on – librarians spent more time searching online. Initially, the same work was done, except that powerful new searching tools became available for reference tasks. No longer were librarians limited to one, two or three access points: now there could be as many access points as there were indexed terms.

Online access brought an explosion of indexing and abstracting. The ability to search every word of an abstract opened additional ways to decide what sources were available. Boolean logic and other search techniques opened new ways to access information. Using these techniques, topics could be combined and a search for information need not be limited to a single topic. A skilled searcher can find information more quickly and better using online electronic sources. As online databases expanded they began to supersede the printed materials. With the introduction of full-text searching end-users can directly access large databases that contain the full text of documents, and do not just point to where a document can be found. The introduction of front-end systems makes it possible for a user to have the full power of search techniques without learning the search requirements for each database.

The end-user can directly access information, without the assistance of an intermediary. Initially librarians argued that no novice could match the power of the sophisticated searcher. This was certainly true initially, as a special language was often required to use the system fully. As search tools improve, knowledge of the subject being searched is often more important than knowing the search techniques. An experienced searcher with knowledge of the subject will almost always search better than an inexperienced searcher with the same knowledge. However, as additional tools were added to assist searchers familiar with the subject, the importance of the intermediary diminishes. Increasingly, the emerging role of the information professional is to train subject specialists in search techniques and, where possible, to design and automate the search process. The librarians moved from being an organizer of collections to an enabler.

Online catalogs are now used in every library and the contents of most libraries can be found using a search tool. The printed catalogs have been replaced by online systems and any librarian, anywhere, can add information to the database. As time goes on, however, standard requirements for transferring data are developing, which enables information in one system to move to another. The Internet opens up access to collections throughout the world because there are standard ways to format and communicate information between systems.

The creation of the inverted index provides the same power for online searching as the relational database provided for data processing. The inverted index makes it possible to rapidly search full-text databases as well as descriptive indexes and abstracts.

The development of technologies associated with networking (the Internet) and search tools that can reach across various networks open up collections that once required a personal visit to a physical location where the collection was housed.

Online searching enabled users to access databases from far away and interact directly with them. Online replaced batch technology for text searches and enabled immediate answers to be given to questions without waiting for the computer to process a request.

Online databases grew at an astounding rate, primarily in scientific, technical and business areas. In 1979, when the first issue of Directory of Online Databases was published, there were 400 databases with 221 database producers and 59 providers of online services. By 1986 this had grown to 2901 databases, 1379 producers and 454 online services. In 1986 there were also 35 gateways. In 1991 the figure had risen to 50 266 databases, with 2158 producers, 731 online services and 106 gateways. The number of such professional databases is now well over 5000.[14] Today what was once the online industry is ubiquitous. The number of databases connected in some way to the world wide networks number in the millions or billions.

With the development of the Internet and the possibility for databases to be developed and accessed by local producers, the numbers grew exponentially. Databases expanded beyond the scientific, technical and business areas and there was a dramatic increase in the number of source databases that provide information directly. In the late 1970s an additional unrecognized need became clear – to provide the same type of information access for in-house collections that was available through the online services.

The development of international online services revolutionized the world of librarianship, particularly librarians working for corporations and organizations (often called special librarians). These people often work with small staffs and specialize in meeting the particular needs of the organization by knowing where to find external information. The Special Libraries Association is debating whether to change its name, and decided to add the same tagline as ARMA: the organization of information professionals.

With the advent of online services, external information traditionally supplied to organizations by specialized libraries is now available for staff of the organization. Instead of maintaining a collection, the librarian becomes the information professional who identifies possible sources, trains staff in the use of search techniques, and works with other information professionals to make information available to the organization.

---

[14] Data provided by Carlos A. Cuadra.

Box 6.3 The contemporary librarian

The impact of technology on the work of the librarian was swift and profound. Within only a few years librarians moved from being keepers of collections to being managers of information.

The contemporary librarian must focus on access and meeting customer needs. The reference interview, which is at the heart of the delivery of services in a library, focuses on determining the needs of a customer and not just what they want. This seemingly simple activity requires skill and patience, for most seekers of information begin with a very limited view of what they need.

In the pre-electronic age the librarian knew what was in the collection and where related collections might be found. If the item was not in the collection, it was borrowed (through interlibrary loan) and physically transported from another collection. Now, however, the librarian knows sources located throughout the world and how to track down and find what is needed. The contemporary librarian needs to be generally knowledgeable in the area where the information is being sought.

By using the new technology, the contemporary librarian becomes an information manager, focusing on information external to the organization.

The Special Libraries Association, the professional association of corporate and organization librarians, is debating whether to keep the name "librarian" and has decided to add the same tagline as the records managers to its organizations name: the "organization of information professionals."

The skills of the librarian (identifying customer needs and knowing where and how to find things) are part of the skills needed for the corporate memory manager.

Once inaccessible or difficult-to-find sources are becoming available to large audiences. Initially, online services simply provided a quicker way to access indexes and other bibliographic sources available on paper. Now, online databases enable users to access valuable information directly.

It is difficult to remember that the need for online access to information was not widely recognized in the early 1970s. Yet end-users, those who actually need and use information, are increasingly accessing online sources generally without the assistance of a professional searcher acting as an intermediary. The initial online databases focused on external information – the information provided by librarians. An increasing number of organizations are taking the information they collect and, using software developed for online databases, organizing internal data and information for online access, both to those within the organization and to others. Information that was once primarily of value within an organization is becoming a valuable commodity – a resource of the organization. More and more organizations are identifying information as an important product. As a result, the tools and techniques once used to access and manage external sources of information are being used to manage internal information as well.

Archivists

Archivists generally concentrate on older material that is on paper. In an organizational or corporate setting, the archivist is the keeper of the permanent records. There have always been some permanent records of an organization: its Charter, minutes of Board meetings and annual reports are typically of historical interest. Relatively few organizations have a designated archivist, but it is clear that the development of a corporate memory system requires identifying strategies to keep the permanent records of the organization properly. This is the traditional domain of the archivist.

Automation is at an early stage in the archival profession, but many of the tools developed by librarians and records managers are applicable to the work of the archivist. In addition to storing and retrieving infor-

---

Box 6.4 The contemporary archivist

The contemporary archivist is involved in the creation of information and not just the storage of documents of historical value. The archivist, like the records manager, must deal with information in a number of media, which may be fragile. Photographs and films are particularly difficult to manage, for the chemicals used have changed over the years and generally require special environments for storage.

Archivists are becoming increasingly involved in devising activities to properly document the actions of an organization. The archivist needs to be involved in the creation of electronic information and not just wait for it to be delivered when it is no longer active. The distinction between active and inactive information is blurred in the electronic environment. The skills of the archivist – identifying and preserving information – are important for the corporate memory manager.

mation, however, the archivist is concerned with the organization as it develops over time. The archivist brings a historical perspective to the institution. Technology enables the information stored and managed by archivists to become available to staff in the organization, and not just to historians who have no connection with the organization. The arrival of automated technology into the archive enables the retrieval of information independent of the principle of provenance, or the order in which materials are created. In the development of the corporate memory system, whether information has historical value is one of the criteria for determining what is kept. Here is where the archivist can bring special skills and techniques to the process of developing the corporate memory. The archivist is skilled at identifying what kinds of documentation are useful and at helping the organization develop systems that will endure over a long period of time. Archivists are used to dealing with information created in many different eras using many different technologies. Having a corporate memory system will also fundamentally transform the work of the archivist, from being an outsider looking into an organization to being an integral part of its activities.

Many archivists see themselves primarily as cultural workers rather than knowledge workers. Thus the relationship between records management and archive management is sometimes strained. The records manager normally looks at information content from the viewpoint of the organization, rather than at the intrinsic value of documents. The archivist has a broader view, often looking at the interests of the historian or the social value of the information beyond the interest of the organization. A corporate memory system requires the perspective of both the archivist and the records manager. A strategy for building a corporate memory system needs to look beyond the immediate self-interest of the organization and see how information may be of value to society at large. The archivist understands the importance of a documentation strategy, that is, an active plan to identify what activities in the organization need to be documented.

The archive profession has much to give to the development of the corporate memory. It is an old and honored profession, often closely tied to the history profession. Many of the archivist's techniques for storing and recording information can be used to develop automated systems to manage the corporate memory.

The term digital archives comes from the world of the archivists – those folks who worry about and deal with information that is of permanent value.

To claim that something is of "permanent" value requires some hubris, but there are those who make those judgments for a living. The archival profession grew out of, and to a considerable extent, is still governed by the needs of the historians. The archivist gathers and preserves the "historical record" – the essential evidence of what happened.

For the past several centuries this work has gone on in the paper world. Archives were, by and large, generally fairly stable collections. The job of the archivist was to "describe" collections by developing "Finding Aids" — ways to enable the scholar and the historian to wend his or her way through a mass of documents.

The organizing principle of the archival profession – that of "provenance"[15] assured that the material, once brought under control, could be examined by future scholars in the same context in which it was collected.

ISO Standard 15489 adopted in 2001 specifically says that it "does not include the management of archival records within archival institutions." (1.1)

An Archival Collection

An archive is a collection of information. It is a nice term, for it can refer both to the place where this collection is held and to the collection itself. An archive is generally part of an institution designed to preserve records for people or organizations that do not create them.

Archivists, then, look at corporate memory from a somewhat different perspective than records managers or businesses. Records were once seen, and by some still are seen, as a sub-set of archives – and in many countries archives control records management. The function of records management, from the traditional archival perspective, is to identify and turn over records of historical value to an archival collection.

A collection of information embodies a purpose – a reason for information of a particular kind to be in the same "place" – to be collected together. In the paper world, an information collection, of which an archive is one example, is literally collected up and brought together. Pieces of paper are identified, marked, indexed and organized in a manner appropriate to a collection.

Collecting and maintaining an archive in paper form is very expensive, for paper must be preserved and housed under carefully controlled conditions.

---

[15] Provenance is defined in the Society of American Archivists Handbook as: or Schellenberg)

Preservation of collections is at the heart of the archival profession – and the caring and maintaining of collections often overwhelms other issues, such as the use of the information being cared form. In the end properly preserved.

Preserving for Re-Use

When we look at a document as a verb – as an activity or process to justify a knowledge belief, then digital archives become a much more dynamic institution — they become more than a collection. They are a set of interpretations – answers to questions.

Archival management has often been linked to the professions of historians – indeed for many archives the primary use (or at least the preferred user) of archives is the professional historian.[16] But historians, even more than other professionals, know that doing history is not a one time thing. It is a dynamic activity which changes depending on our point of view – even our culture and tradition.

An archives designed to serve the knowledge age cannot be a static institution either. It needs to serve the needs of a community of practice.

A dynamic view of digital archives aligns it much more with the tradition of documentation – where document is a verb that encompasses the activities that go into identifying and preserving a body of knowledge for a community of practice. In this sense a digital archives is at the heart of preserving corporate memory — and goes far beyond preserving records.

Corporate memory, as we have seen, is the information that is kept for re-use by an organization. The organizing principle for a corporate memory collection is its use for an organization. There may be other uses for this same collection. Perhaps the information is of historical value – that is perhaps it is of value to those outside the organizations.

Historians have a particularly interest in archives, for without archival collections they cannot do their work. In fact, most archival theory (and practice) has traditionally been driven by the needs of historians, not by the needs of the organization creating the records.

Corporate memory collections, that information of value for re-use, puts the focus on the organizational and business uses of the collection, not on its historical value.

---

[16] The genealogist, rather than the historian, has become the primary user of official government archives in the Untied States – a fact treated with ambivalence by many "serious"archivists.

Records Managers and Archivists

Records managers and archivists look at the world – and the collections of information to which they relate – from different perspectives. Records managers come to the information from the world of the business and the organization. They are often overwhelmed by the problems of identifying and capturing information as it floods through an organization. The records manager, in the end, worries about how to get rid of information – so that the really essential evidence – the information of value for re-use – can be captured.

The records managers capture. The archivists preserve. When it comes to digital archives, however, the two approaches/disciplines converge. Digital archives are not necessarily physical collections – in fact most digital archives are not brought together in a single place and preserved as an interconnected entity.

As we saw above, a document in the digital environment is a verb . . . it is an answer to a question. What makes a document a part of corporate memory is the context in which the question is asked . . . who asks it and for what purpose. Whether or not documents are preserved in a document form is not essential in the digital world, as it is in the paper world. As long as the elements can be pulled together to answer the question, then the document is preserved.

The move to digital archives is not, therefore, just a move from one medium (paper) to another (digits). It calls into question the fundamental principle that underlies archival management – that information/documents must be preserved in their original order. Digital documents, as a matter of fact, are not normally kept . . . let alone preserved . . . in the order that they are displayed. The flexibility that is inherent in digital archives comes from the way in which information is kept.

Digital archives also call into question the fundamental principles of records management – assumptions on inventories and disposition schedules that underlie the practice of the profession.

Anyone interested in preserving corporate memory has much to learn from digital archivists. As fields merge and overlap, distinctions that were once thought to be important pale into insignificance. How we preserve corporate memory can be learned from the digital archivists. The tools and methodologies to capture what archivist call institutional memory apply to corporate memory.

CHAPTER SEVEN

The technologies

The technologies that accelerated the loss of corporate memory in an electronic environment also offer solutions. The development of a corporate memory system is primarily a management problem, not a technological problem. Technology facilitated the shift of records to electronic form. This is not the first, nor will it be the last, shift in media for the corporate memory. Writing meant that memory could move beyond the oral tradition; stone tablets were replaced by manuscripts made of various animal and vegetable products; the printing press transformed the media in which information was kept; carbon paper, copying machines and microfilm all changed the media in which the corporate memory resided.

Electronic data and documents can be viewed, therefore, as the next step in technology. We need to look at the various technologies, which are often unstable – certainly more usable than stone tablets and generally less stable than paper records. As we move into the technology dominated by electronic information, the tools to manage these documents, records and data are developing. We need to integrate existing technologies to develop systems to manage the corporate memory – and corporate memory systems that will be open to evolving and new technologies.[17]

---

[17] In the first edition of this book I said, "Of all the chapters in this book, this one is the most likely to be outdated by the time it is read. A book, after all, requires years to develop, write, publish and distribute. It is an appropriate way to convey knowledge and theories – ways of looking at things – but is not, by its nature, an efficient way to convey the state of technology." With a decade's worth of hindsight, probably the understanding of how our work can be different has altered even more than the technologies, which were often at an early stage, but have not changed substantially in the last decade. Relatively few changes were needed in this chapter for this revised edition.

The key to a successful corporate memory system is the ability to retrieve meaningful documents and information. This requires a system for marking documents and a way to find information using those markers. Substantial improvements in the ability to retrieve documents electronically enable us to develop a corporate memory management system using electronic tools.

Sometimes we need to describe items only well enough to locate them. For example, a locator index to image files may be a good choice for personnel files if the anticipated use is to retrieve a staff member's folder as a whole. If we are interested in always retrieving a folder, all we need is a unique identifier for each one: a name, social security number, a department or other information. Imaging systems initially adopted the traditional way of organizing documents into folders, even if they did not need to be organized this way, because our ways of thinking about records are rooted in the paper-based system.

However, a minimal locator index is insufficient when looking for information that is inside the folder. It is not sufficient, for example, to find the folders for all staff members who had worked on a particular project during a given period of time – or for all staff members with a particular skill or experience. Many systems provide only a few fields, such as contract, project, report numbers and, perhaps, part of a title. This might be adequate for inventory control but is woefully inadequate for content-based retrieval, for example, to find all reports on a particular topic, or prepared by a certain individual or set of authors. In order to manage the corporate memory, we need to do more than locate documents: we need to be able to retrieve them quickly in the format in which they are needed. Retrieval based on the content of the information in documents is a key requirement of the corporate memory.

Requirements for the corporate memory system

Many automated information management systems can effectively track documents, whether these are in paper form or images. Such systems are not, however, designed to deal with the mass of wordprocessed documents being produced by organizations. Most database management systems do not capture source information at the time when it is created, have limited text retrieval capabilities, and have no retention or scheduling mechanisms. These systems work in a world in which a document is clearly defined and preserved in a physical form that can be stored and recreated. Unfortunately most corporate memory does not reside in these forms.

The requirements for a corporate memory system include:

1. Descriptive systems that move from one level of description to another. In other words, the descriptions of the content of a document need to be moved along with the document if it is moved to another file folder.
2. The description of the information in the system needs to be enriched as the corporate memory system is used. Searches need to be saved so they may be reused or modified for later inquiries. We need to be able to apply the results of one search for use in subsequent searches.
3. A single interface is needed to access the corporate memory. Even though the information system will consist of a number of systems, in various media at various sites, access to the information should be through a single system interface.
4. The transformation of the work process. This is necessary to justify the cost of the technological improvements. A number of technological developments have converged to make the management of corporate memory not only a possibility, but a reality.

Browsing and searching

Searching focuses on finding specific items, and automation greatly increases the ability of a user to find an item. Often, however, a person is not looking for a particular item, but rather is learning about a subject or an area of information. Very often we do not even know what question we want to ask, let alone know a particular document that would be the answer to the question. In a library, books that are about the same subject are located together. Such a system encourages the user to go to a physical area and see what might be near a known subject. In order to fully meet the needs of information seekers, electronic searching and retrieval systems will not only need to be able to search for specific items, but also browse through a field of knowledge. A professional information searcher is often best equipped to find a particular item, but a browser needs only to know the subject being investigated and to learn more about it as browsing continues. Browsing is a learning activity; searching is a discovery of objects.[18] Effective retrieval often requires a combina-

---

[18] Barry Wheeler pointed out the distinction between browsing and searching. Sheryl Rosenthal, an expert searcher, shows how browsing-like results can come from improved search systems. Both agree that there are 'browsers' and 'searchers' in the world, and that 'searchers' look for items and 'browsers' look for information pointers to information, but also the information itself. It is no longer necessary for an end-user to go through a professional to identify material

tion of browsing and searching. The learning inherent in browsing is enabled as electronic browsers become more and more powerful.

As telecommunications technology develops the possibility of transferring larger and larger amounts of data online grows. The ability to directly link and access databases stored in remote computers, opens up new possibilities to link information stored in many different locations and search across disparate collections in a multitude of locations.

The use of Boolean logic and other tools of inquiry for searching and retrieval greatly increase the recall and precision of searches. These technological advances enable the searcher to find not only pointers to information, but also the information itself. It is no longer necessary for an end-user to go through a professional to identify material of interest: users can search directly in online databases. Even though a user's skills might not match those of the information professionals, their knowledge of the material they are searching and the ability to interact directly with the information proves to be of immense value. Online searching is becoming universalized and opens the possibility of developing sophisticated information systems to manage the corporate memory.

Enabling technologies

The development of searching techniques is just one of the enabling technologies for the corporate memory system. Others include:

* powerful desktop and laptop computing;
* inexpensive memory;
* improved software;
* new interfaces, such as point and click;
* inexpensive storage;
* efficient telecommunications, including high-speed modems;
* local and wide area networks.
* Automated browsers

In order to fully utilize the power of these tools, an integrated digital environment is needed – one in which there is immediate access to information needed to do work. These enabling technologies have developed gradually over the past generation. Their power comes from integration, which enables information management to move into the digital age.

Initially, automation required large numbers of technicians in order to develop applications. The microcomputer brought the power of the computer to the desk, and the networking of these powerful tools opened up communication possibilities. The development of communication technologies abolishes the distinction between internal and external information and provides for the development of the corporate memory system.

These technologies are becoming commonplace in most organizations. What is needed is the will and ability to integrate technologies to transform the workplace. The technology is generally available off the shelf, and the major costs are in the integration of systems, the training of staff and the proper design of workflow.

Relational and inverted index systems

The two basic types of search software package are relational and inverted index systems. Most programmers are familiar with and most comfortable with relational systems, which were initially built to handle numeric data, fixed-length text fields and date fields. Today many in-house mainframe systems are designed to use relational systems.

Inverted index systems, however, were built to handle large amounts of text by creating an alphanumeric index of searchable terms as data are entered. Searchable terms may include words or phrases (or both) from such field information as title, company name, date, abstract or full text. Such systems often have variable-length fields and records in order to be able to accommodate the needs of text-based systems, which have to deal with the vagaries and varieties of language.

The inverted index contains pointers to the actual documents, so that when a search is executed the system does not need to search through each document: it simply goes to the index and follows the pointers. The main advantage of an inverted file system is response time. Search tools should not require the user to choose specific databases for searching, nor should they require the learning of different search techniques for different databases. These tools should enable the searcher to access multiple information sources.

Until recently, databases external to an organization were generally accessed only by information professionals, who were trained to know not only the content of the various databases but also the various means by which they are accessed. As these database systems have become more generally available, usually via commercial vendors, powerful new search tools have been developed. Searching is no longer the purview of the information professional. What is still important, however, is human intervention to improve and make searching more successful for members of a community. The expertise of the professional searcher adds value and refinement to the search tools.

Thesauri and Communities

Knowledge resides in communities of practice. The knowledge of one person is information to another. Finding that information requires the use of language – and languages are based in communities. The same word can mean many different things in different situations – even if we are speaking the "same" language. We can post a letter, post an entry into an accounting system, post a notice on a bulletin board or go to the post office.

   Maximum retrieval that is precise is enabled through the use of thesauri – structured terms that are based in languages of communities. The widespread use of thesauri came with the on-line industry where the considerable cost of developing specialized thesauri was justified.

   There cannot be a "universal thesaurus" good for all searchers. Each thesaurus is rooted in the practice of a community. Precise retrieval is greatly enhanced when controlled vocabularies are used. Automated corporate memory system, to be most effective, need to adopt thesauri and other controlled vocabulary and authority file techniques.

Accessing multiple databases

Solutions are being developed, often by a team that includes an information manager and end-users working together to search multiple databases. The main requirement is that search tools should demand little or no knowledge of a specific search protocol. Access should be guided

---

Knowledge arises not out of the particular activity of one person, but the collective work of the community. The conditions for collaboration are created in communities of practice. Of course, an individual is the source of knowledge, but the development of a body of knowledge and how any particular part of that body fits with the whole, takes place within a community. Knowledge is not just a piece, but part of a whole picture of reality.

Megill, Thinking for a Living, p. 109

Box 7.1 The inverted index

The inverted index makes searching large text databases possible. Using such an index, information can be found without physically going through a file in sequence. The technology is used in many text searching systems accompanying wordprocessing software, and many image systems.

An inverted index is an index of every occurrence of a term and its location on the computer. Unlike with a traditional index, which applies one or two terms to a document, every word is indexed, so that a document can be accessed by any term in it, by a combination of such terms and by terms located adjacent to or near each other. When a search is conducted, therefore, it is not necessary to search sequentially through the entire text, but rather the index terms using Boolean logic. The searcher can ask where two terms both appear in the same document (A N D) or where one or more terms appear (O R). Other criteria can be applied, such as proximity (how close two terms are two each other).

Since the entire database does not need to be searched, searching can be carried out much faster than using other technologies. Since an inverted index can be generated automatically, it is not necessary for someone to manually index every document, although additional terms (descriptors) can be given to a document that then becomes part of the index.

A system using an inverted index and Boolean searching often eliminates the need to manually index and abstract most documents—both costly and time-consuming activities. It opens up the full range of an organization's information for access. It also enables the traditional activities, such as indexing and abstracting of documents to be carried on when the added time is warranted. This is particularly important for information that has very long-term value with language that may not capture the full meaning of the document and to which additional descriptors increase access to the information.

It is important to note that this technology is not dependent on the physical storing of documents as a single entity. It is applicable to the 'new document' assembled upon request.

The index is called inverted because it enables us to index all terms and not just a few chosen terms as we must do in a traditional paper filing system or manual library card catalog. By using Boolean logic, the searcher can then conduct searches that ask for documents (locations) by searching the index, rather than through the entire file.

by the user's thought processes and the specific characteristics of the information being sought. For example, an opening screen can provide information about what is available to search, as well as information on whom to call for additional help or on how to enter suggestions. The next set of menu screens might ask the searcher to select the type of search to be executed, e.g. full text, subject/index terms, particular number etc. The actual search screens provide 'fill-in-the blank' type options, perhaps in a query-by-form format, that utilize the entire range of available full-text search features underneath the menu, transparent to the user. Additional screens ask the searcher to choose the format of the displayed or printed report, e.g. titles only, full patent/trademark information, images etc. All of these menus are accompanied by context-sensitive help screens.

Desk-top scanning

The cost of using optical character recognition (OCR) scanning to capture text in ASCII format is rapidly declining. The availability of desktop scanners and scanners integrated into copy machines provides flexibility for interfacing with other OCR software and makes the distribution of work-flow processes across departments possible. As a result, decisions can be made at a level where knowledge is available to support intelligent decisions.

If the full text of documents is captured through OCR, records may still need to be enhanced with descriptive information, such as assigned subjects or keywords. Information retrieval is greatly enhanced by this. The level of description and the form in which information is stored are driven by the nature of the material. The evaluation of information will determine how it is managed, how long it is kept and the proper level of description.

Standard generalized markup language[19]

Although the shift from paper to electronic-based documentation systems threatens the traditional ways of capturing corporate memory, it opens

---

[19] XML and its various forms and derivatives have blossomed since the first edition of this book was written in the mid 1990's. SGML is the basis for the developed of these standardized ways to make and apply metadata to documents.

the way for the development of corporate memory management systems. With the development of the standard generalized markup language (SGML) new possibilities in document publication, distribution, access and retrieval were opened for corporate memory management.

SGML is a system of codes for tagging the elements of a document using a standard structure and command language to facilitate the presentation of information across computer platforms. The decomposition of the document into its structural elements is the foundation of SGML. It enables the receiving computer to recognize what is the title, where paragraphs begin, what is a graphic, and so on. SGML was initially developed to enable publishers to send marked-up text across various computer platforms and various publishing or wordprocessing packages. It provides the basis for searching across various platforms.

Search tools

Search tools are currently available to enable access to numerous sources of information via a single entry point. These searches can be transparent to the end-user and access both internal and external databases. The available technology enables search interfaces to be created and modified at the workgroup level, or to meet the requirements of specific groups of customers.

Since the contents of the corporate memory might include many images, such as graphics and photographs, imaging must be a part of any satisfactory search and retrieval system. A strong search engine to retrieve images must be an important part of a corporate memory management system.

In early systems, images were retrieved by image ID or some other identifying number. By integrating a full-text search engine into the corporate memory management system, it is possible to have content based retrieval and, by implication, retrieval of a much more precise and relevant set of information.

The textual descriptions and other pieces of fielded information contained in records are, by their very nature, subject to change. The underlying database management software should allow data created in other software package types, e.g. wordprocessing files, to be added to a record on request. This requires running data through an appropriate filter or conversion program and automatically uploading and appending them to the matching record. The system should also automatically enter the ID of the requesting staff member and the date and time of the activity.

An audit trail should be provided so that supervisory remarks, reviews or approvals can be traced to specific people. This feature is particularly important to establish the history of the development of a document. State-of-the-art search systems come with a wide variety of features and protocols. For example, some use Boolean logic, others fuzzy logic, others a combination of the two. Some systems provide a 'Soundex'-type capability that allows the user to enter terms and have the system map those terms to terms that sound similar.

Systems can provide a 'supersearch' capability that takes subject terms entered and matches them against a subject authority file, adding related terms to the strategy. The advantage is that users do not have to become familiar with the controlled vocabulary used to index the database. This is another example of transparent searching.

A feature that is being used by an increasing number of search systems is relevance ranking. The point of this is to rank the retrieved documents in a 'relevant' order, so that the search strategy can be expanded to locate similar documents using terms that may not have been used in the original source.

Natural language searching is another option, but one needs to be careful to determine what the search system really means by natural language. If language searching does not use any kind of artificial intelligence but simply uses the tool of relevance ranking to search for similar documents, all words in the query are used in the algorithm. This means that if a searcher enters the query 'look for toilet seats in the title' the system will throw out all stop-list words and search on the remaining

---

Box 7.2 Supersearch

Imagine a records management application involving the names of departments. With a control (authority) file reflecting the history of department/unit name changes over time, we could, for example, enter departments such as HR or human resources and find records indexed under Human Resources and also those indexed under Personnel, and any other former names for that department or unit.

In this example the searcher does not need to know all of the various names of the departments in order to carry out the search. This memory of historical name changes can be built into the search system.

Similarly, it would be possible to search by functions that may have moved from one unit to another if the appropriate historical changes can be determined.

terms. This means that the initial set of retrieval documents will include the word 'title' in the document.

Regardless of the search features employed by the software, search screens and menus can and should be modifiable by the user to reflect the specific requirements of each workgroup. Authorized users who have access to data in databases used for specific purposes (such as client billing records, manufacturing, inventories or clinical records) can now get to the information in these disparate databases by using powerful text retrieval tools to store, access and disseminate information available in the corporate memory database. This can bring information together from multiple sources, both within and outside the organization, to meet the information needs of the user.

Scripts

Scripts enable previous retrievals in the corporate memory to be saved and made available for future searchers. The increase in retrievability of information relies on the use of scripts to retrieve information based upon frequently asked questions, which can be stored and reused. Scripts can be created that are either a series of saved search strategies or, more creatively, a series of saved steps that allow the searcher to interact by filling in their requirements at specified points. This type of request could then be translated by the software and used to activate searches on multiple platforms, all transparent to the user after the initial interaction. Search results can be delivered by sorting the hits according to the system and database searched, and duplicates could either be grouped together or eliminated.

The success of this approach requires an understanding of what searchers in each workgroup need. Searchers should always be given the option to enter search strategies 'their way,' i.e. using system protocol, if desired, and selecting systems and databases without any software intervention.

It is not really necessary for users to go through complex multistep processes to log on to a system. Systems exist that log a user in after asking for an ID and a password. Menus can be designed so that after the user has entered the above information, by selecting a vendor, database or script they can be automatically logged into the appropriate system, internal or external. These same menus can provide access to other systems or to the Internet, for example, through hypertext links.

The Internet

The explosive growth of the Internet made online searching available to many more people and dramatically decreased the cost of access to information online. The development of minicomputers and multiuser microcomputer systems, combined with Internet access, removed the need to store information in large, centralized collections.

The Internet uses all of the technologies discussed above. The corporate memory system can use these same techniques and, when put properly into place, will enable an organization to access information anywhere on the Internet, as well as enabling others to access information belonging to that organization.

The genius of the tools developed by the online industry is shown by the way they are applied to the use of the Internet. Particularly important is the development of means by which a searcher can move from concept to concept using hypertext and other tools. This means that surrogates – records which point to documents – are no longer necessary, and information can be managed and accessed in accordance with its content.

The Internet opens a way to increase the corporate memory's value as a major asset. Obviously, some parts of the corporate memory will not be allowed outside the organization, but many parts may well have value to others, which could result in new products for the organization and new services to its customers.

Bringing the World Wide Web in-house

The distributed information systems based on the concept of the World Wide Web (to include the Internet) provide one information model on how the corporate memory can be organized.[20] The World Wide Web, with hypertext links that can take us to computers located anywhere in the world, can be applied equally well to in-house networks and to the management of the corporate memory.

The development of GUIs makes the use of the various technologies more intuitive. Different hardware and software are typically needed to manage different parts of an organization. Financial management systems are designed to manage money. Database systems designed to handle financial data (spreadsheets) are not well suited to managing text, and

---

[20] Much of this discussion is taken from an unpublished paper presented by Judith Wanger at the Online Conference in 1995.

text management systems don't crunch numbers nearly as well as financial database management systems do.

Rather than forcing information to fit within the constraints of a package designed for another type of information and process, the Web model focuses on interfaces that permit a diverse set of programs and files to be linked. Programs can be launched by any standard Web server resident on the host system, and they allow for services to be requested from software. Each software developer writes their own interface. Once this is written, full interactive browsing sessions for Web users are provided.

As an example, take a simple corporate memory database with the following references:

- records which reference searches that have been performed on one or more systems;
- another set of records that describes images of line drawings and photos from several different departments. In addition to a summary description, each individual image file has its own annotation or notes: for example, a front view of a building;
- other records in the corporate memory database describe individual records or batches of records being managed through other software.

Each workstation would have preferences set to specify the helper application or viewer to be used for the various classes of files. For example, some files might use the browser itself as a viewer, whereas others might require specialized viewers provided by desktop publishing or wordprocessing software.

Retrieving from the corporate memory

Information is retrieved from the corporate memory in the following manner.

- The user forms a request for information from the text management database in the corporate memory database. This enables the full power of text searching tools to be used in formulating the request. Standardized languages and alternative search terms can be automatically brought into the search by reference to thesauri, tables of organizational structure with alternative names over time, and other standard information that will ensure that the search is formulated to retrieve the full range of information needed.

- The database of previous searches is evaluated using all the automated tools available, to see if the same or similar searches have been done before. There are two reasons for this:
  1) Most requested information has been asked for before. If this is a repetition of a previous search, the software can note that the information is needed once again and who needs it. This will help determine the worth of information.
  2) Information may be linked to other information in unexpected ways. Information in a database may be needed elsewhere in the organization for a different purpose than the original one.

Even if an identical request has not been made before, similar requests may be available. These will help the user identify additional information that might be useful. This is similar to the process used in online searching, where information about previous searches helps make linkages in unexpected ways.

Once the search is formulated (this is, by and large, an automated process), the required information is retrieved. Each record in the search report includes a link to the file of stored search results located in a particular directory. The proper command is issued and the retrieved file is sent to the user's workstation.

Changing technologies

The shift from paper-based documents to the first generation of electronically stored information (flat-file format) stored primarily on large centralized machines evolved over approximately a 20-year period. The shift from a predominately flat-file structure to a relational database structure took approximately 8 years. The move from a predominately mainframe technology to a technology using clients and servers took only about 4 years. We are now involved in a major shift from physical collections of documents to documents that are assembled in response to a query. As information moves closer to the workplace, the importance of minicomputers, which often serve as the most logical host for the corporate memory, increases once again.

The increasing speed of change in technology makes it even more important that the corporate memory system be created so that the information can migrate through changes in the organization's technology. Using software that makes it easy and seamless to log on to and search multiple systems and databases, without knowledge of searching skills, means that staff will be able to meet expectations for searching and finding related information.

The solution to the problem of managing corporate memory is to identify all information worth keeping and apply currently available technology to its management. This means that the corporate memory management system needs to span the currently available technologies, and also be open to the development of newer areas. This openness to change must be an integral part of any solution.

The goal of the corporate memory system is to allow access to information that is dispersed across network devices, operating systems and applications, thus taking advantage of the best that technology has to offer.

The move from one technology to another does not happen all at once. Even when the basic form in which information is stored changes, much of the information of value to the organization is not transferred to the new medium. The organization is thus faced with information stored in both the old and the new ways. There are three possible courses of action in such a situation:

- ignore or discard the information using the old technology;
- convert the information to the new technology;
- creates a software bridge between old and new.

To maintain a constant information structure across technological generational boundaries is difficult. If a document is constructed across the generations of technology, how are information elements stored in an earlier generation related to new and evolved information elements that are stored in later generations? These logical problems are compounded by physical problems such as incompatible storage media, inability to run old software, or old data.

As information from within and without the organization is integrated, additional technologies enter the picture. For example, when staff members are called upon to use information contained in external databases they must not only learn how to use new machines, but must learn entirely new techniques for processing information that were once the purview of other professionals. Therefore, the corporate memory management system must be able to manage information from a multitude of information systems in varying stages of technology, as well as various types of information differently, depending on its value. In order to do this, information will need to be described at different levels and be moved from one level of description to another.

In summary, different information requires different levels of description, ranging from simple indexes, from an index with an abstract, to a full text and an index. The question of how far to carry such description requires a sense of the company's information needs. The information contained in the corporate memory, however, is of varying value: the more valuable requires more description. To make the matter even more complex, information may be extremely valuable at one point in time and of little or no value at another.

CHAPTER EIGHT

Performance Centered Learning

In order to develop a corporate memory system it is necessary to introduce new technologies into the organization and teach the staff how to use existing technologies more effectively. More than traditional training is required: learning in a technological environment is becoming more and more important as traditional training turns out to be expensive and, often, transitory. Organizations are beginning to look at various ways to solve the problem of introducing technology into the workplace. Our goal must continue to be to integrate information whenever possible and make it accessible to those who need it.[21]

Traditional training

Too often, when new technologies are introduced the workflow is changed to meet the requirements of the software. A software package is identified, purchased and introduced into the organization. Trainers are then hired to teach the software application. In the traditional training environment, a trainer who is familiar with the new technology is brought in to teach staff how it can be used. However, the trainer is not usually

---

[21] Barry Wheeler contributed many of the ideas in this chapter. Since the first edition of this book in 1997, I have had the privilege of working with Noel Dickover, who has taught me much about how a performance-centered learning environment can be created. See http://www.communibuild.com/

familiar with the work situation and generally leaves its specific application up to the students. There is also often a time lapse – sometimes very long – between training and the actual implementation of a technology.

The introduction of new technology enables changes in the work process, so that much of what has already been learned becomes obsolete once the technology is fully implemented. Users are normally left on their own, with generic documentation and access to a help desk, and often make use of only a small percentage of the capabilities of the technology. However, there is a better way to introduce technology to an organization.

Learning

The trouble with traditional training is that it does not enable the user to learn about the product over time, and to take control of the technology. The technology, not the user, determines how it is used. The power of modern technology, however, is only fully unleashed when the user masters it and uses it in new and unexpected ways. Learning how to use technology must be based on an understanding that people learn in a context over time.

Learning is a student's activity; training and education are often done from the viewpoint of the instructor. An organization needs to become a learning organization – one in which the acquisition of new skills and knowledge is a normal part of life. Learning, like any other activity, takes time and commitment, and in this chapter we will discuss how an organization can develop the type of learning environment that is necessary to implement a corporate memory system.

Implementing a corporate memory management system with adequate computer search and retrieval technologies requires significant changes in work processes and thought processes. The workflow of the organization will change over time. Such changes should not be required by the software but should arise out of new possibilities for improved customer service.

In other words, information systems should support business activities, not create new work. Staff will need to learn new ways of doing business. Learning is best done in context: 'just-in-time learning' that is available when and where a new skill is needed. Much more is needed than simply training to use a tool.

Computer technology is used by workers at all levels of an organization and frequently changes the way in which tasks are done. In addition, automating certain activities may hide work functions and make it difficult for the worker to see all the activities that take place.

The pace of change ads to the problem: systems may be introduced and replaced within a single working year. No sooner is one system learned than it is replaced by one using different commands to perform more complex tasks. This means that most training programs will be inadequate. Workers will need sufficient expertise and the flexibility to respond and adapt to the required changes of complex new environments. Traditional training and education will continue to have a role, but should be integrated into the learning environment that encourages the staff to assimilate new skills and techniques at the most appropriate time. Learning cannot be optional: if a corporate memory system is to work individual staff members cannot be allowed to decide whether or not to use it. Information appropriate for the corporate memory belongs to the organization and needs to be managed as a corporate resource.

Individual staff members will need to make decisions that determine the value of documents. They will need to identify the type of document and appropriate keywords (subject terms or descriptors) to describe it. Such decisions can be simplified by providing each staff member with clearly defined choices that can be made easily and quickly. Only then can privacy be protected while the corporate memory is used to its fullest extent. In the end, staff must take responsibility for what goes into the corporate memory and provide the appropriate description. Staff will also learn how to use the power of the corporate memory to improve their work. Over time, the value of the corporate memory system will grow as the information contained therein expands.

Minimize training and support

The successful introduction of technology that encourages the improvement of work processes requires the development of systems that minimize the need for training and support. A system should use terms and techniques already used by staff members, and should be designed from the point of view of those who use it. Therefore, members of the work team need to be involved in system development. There are ways to minimize the need for training and support:

1. Use metaphors: Choosing the proper metaphor (one that makes sense to the staff member in a particular situation) means that staff do not need to learn a new language in order to use the technology. Graphic

user interfaces enable systems to represent concepts and structures symbolically, with representations familiar to the users.

2. Rapid prototyping: Current tools allow the development of initial program models and prototypes that approximate closely to the desired user interface. These can then be used as starting points for system development. Involving users directly in their design greatly reduces the amount of training and support subsequently required.

3. Performance support systems: Integrated computer technology provides, on demand, a combination of hypertext help systems and multimedia computer-assisted learning sequences to minimize training.

The information specialist

Experience shows that the best teacher is a peer.[22] Thus, the most effective way to promote the efficient implementation of technology is where one member of the workgroup teaches the others.

- The ultimate integration of work, technology and learning, however, will be in teams comprising both task and information technology specialists. Such specialists have knowledge of the work being done and also of how to implement technology in the workplace. The term 'information specialist' is used to designate the person responsible for effective implementation of the technology. This responsibility could be shared between a number of staff, and time must be specifically allocated to the job: a new task cannot be added to existing responsibilities. The job description of an information specialist might include:
- participating in prototype and system development. Someone is needed at the workgroup level to develop and implement individualized systems for searching and learning, including work screens, task scripts and other custom modifications that are appropriate for a particular workgroup;
- being responsible for obtaining, installing and configuring support systems and tailoring them to meet the needs of the workgroup;
- providing help desk services for specific tasks as needed.

The information specialist provides training, continuing education and support services at the workgroup level. This extends the current 'train

---

[22] This statement comes from many years as a teacher and educator. It is also supported by educational research which shows that the most effective learning situation is one in which learners and teachers participate together.

the trainer' approach that maximizes the use of instructional resources while distributing expertise and support to each workgroup. A number of other steps can be taken to enable staff to learn how to use the system effectively.

Integrated learning

There is always a trade-off between instructional power and instructional efficiency. A personal instructor, available whenever needed, is always the best way to learn. In order for learning to take place, however, it requires a comfortable atmosphere where staff can play with a new system to learn how it works. Efficiency has traditionally been achieved through large lectures and in uniform learning experiences, but it is clearly impossible to imagine and teach the sequences for every imaginable task. As a result, mass training is inefficient if there are different learning styles and cognitive starting points for each member of the workforce. What appears to be efficient often ends up alienating staff from new technology, which is seen as one more burden to bear rather than a tool to liberate them from drudgery.

Learning, in contrast, takes place where and when it is needed. It is the result of an interaction between a student and a situation. A teacher is important in setting up and structuring a situation in which learning can take place, and in encouraging co-workers to teach each other. Learning is a personal activity and proceeds at various speeds for various people and at various speeds for the same person at different times. An ongoing learning environment is important and is essential for implementing a corporate memory system, whose power comes from the staff having new resources available to improve their work. Thus, the integration of learning with the organization's workflow is essential, and should continue as the corporate memory system develops and changes the workflow.

Tools

The tools to develop a system that integrates learning and support include:

1. Hypertext learning systems: These allow a user to follow links from a known starting point to a specific text, image, audio or video sequence. The starting point may be a table of contents provided by the help system, a wizard invoked at the start of a complex process, or a request

for information after a problem has occurred. The response is directly related to the work context of the request and is delivered directly to the workstation when needed.

2. Instructional delivery systems: These currently include four components:
   - help sequences, which are usually straightforward text sequences, formatted for comprehension and retention to provide specific information upon request. Windows environments provide a hypertext help system that may be modified and extended by the information specialist to meet specific needs;
   - instructional sequences that present simulated tasks and interactive sequences. They may include formatted text, images and work screen sequences, audio and/or full-motion video;
   - wizards that guide a worker through the actual task, step by step. With this help the worker can complete part of an actual job and, in the process, learn how the system operates;
   - hypertext materials that can be mounted on a user's workstation as part of the initial program load and available whenever the program is in use, or may be mounted on a networked server made available to the worker upon demand.

Learning needs to be seen as an ongoing part of the work process, rather than something done in isolation. Learning is internalized when the user wants to know and use a process, not beforehand. When a new procedure or concept is introduced, it needs to be repeated in the work situation and support needs to be given within the work context, for it to be used effectively and thoroughly learned. For this reason, learning is best done when information professionals are involved in the reengineering of the work process that implements the effective use of the new technology.

CHAPTER NINE

Workflow

The introduction of the corporate memory system profoundly changes the way business is done. For example, instead of making copies of documents for distribution, items are placed into the corporate memory system for all appropriate persons to access. The need for copying and the associated filing systems diminishes as the staff becomes comfortable using the corporate memory system. This does not mean that an office becomes paperless: paper copies can be printed out on demand if required. It does mean that information will preferably be stored and exchanged in electronic form, rather than on paper. Paper copies are just that – copies of electronic records that are put on paper for convenience.

The revival of the registry system

When paper was the major medium used to record information, documentation of the activities of the corporation was a routine part of the workflow. At particular points in the work process, when a document was signed off and sent out of the office, a file copy was made. If no document was sent out transactions might be documented by a memo to the file.

The invention of the typewriter and carbon paper enabled multiple copies of documents to be made, some of which were identified as file copies. Filing systems were developed and revolutionized the way in which documentation took place, replacing the registry system in the United States.

ISO standard 15489 recognizes the value of registering documents as they enter into the corporate memory. Registration assigns a unique identifier to a document and puts it within a file plan and retention schedule. When information and records were managed in central file rooms, registration was a normal practice. In some countries (such as Australia) registration continued long aft it had been abandoned in the United States in 1911. Registration remains, even in the United States, for particular documents – as the name of the office the Register of Deeds (the office where land records are kept) implies.

Except for a very few very important records, such as deeds, the ubiquitous copying machine (and its even more ubiquitous e-mail attachment) replaced registration. With enough copies out there, so it seemed, "someone" will always have a copy of what we may need to re-use.

Registering a document is the first step in an automated document management system. Applying a number and placing the document within the context of a system is the first step in determining its value. Fortunately, registration of documents can, to a large extent, be automated.

In the paper-based registry system each document was registered – often in a bound volume that served as an index to the contents of a file room. Documents were normally stored in the order in which they were registered. In modern businesses, however, the files of paper copies were used to document the corporate memory.

Copying replaced registering

The foundation of modern records management lies in the history of managing the explosion of files that came with ever-easier means of copying. Copy machines replaced carbon paper and making more and more copies of documents became the common way to save information.

New filing technologies developed: lateral cabinets, open shelving and compact moveable shelves. Records management became a hopeless chase of identifying the record copy, saving it as long as required and begging organizations to discard the mountain of copies dispersed in file cabinets throughout the company. The collapse of many filing systems is a direct result of a paper-based technology in which the proliferation of copies replaced information management. Most organizations had no effective records management system.

The arrival of electronic files compounded the problem, since copying became even easier and distribution more widespread. The computer also brought about a profound change in the workflow of an organization: Drafts were circulated long before the final version was signed off. With the development of e-mail, informal notes were easily distributed to identify lists of recipients. In sum, the file copy was never made. The corporate memory system is a resurrection of certain aspects of the registry system, and the designation of a document as a part of the corporate memory is one way of registering it as important to the organization.

Management information systems

When management information systems (MIS) began storing information electronically, the first areas to be automated were the routine activities of a business. In designing applications the developers closely mirrored the traditional manual tasks: although there were no paper files to put in folders, the applications were developed as if there were, and the information was collected and stored as discrete units in electronic form. These discrete units were called records, and a set of related records was called a file. Although the actual electronic files were normally stored in a centralized computer, they were divided according to department. The same information was often kept by the various departments and paper copies continued to be kept for most records. Instead of simplifying record keeping, dual systems were created: the computer was used to process information that was normally maintained on paper or on microfilm, and multiple electronic records and files were created. As the process of automation continued, more and more information was kept only in electronic form and the document structure based on the paper model began to disintegrate. The process was imperceptible at first, but was greatly accelerated as data began to be exchanged in electronic form. Advances in data entry, imaging, optical character recognition and other related technologies changed the way in which work was done, creating new possibilities and requirements. In the process of automation, needs change and many tasks become redundant. As more and more parts of the organization become automated, massive savings can be made, thereby paying the costs of automation.

As the organization shifts from automating existing processes to using technology to work in an entirely new way, we move beyond the departmental management of information. A corporate memory system gives users at both department and enterprise level access to all appropriate information, regardless of its location. As a result, workers are empowered at the lowest possible level. As information is identified and managed as an asset of the entire organization, and not just the particular department or unit that initially created, it begins to be recycled and reused.

Integrating information

The distinction between internally generated materials and acquired materials vanishes as information becomes digitized and available beyond the department level. Individual technologies, developed for specific purposes, come together and are integrated. Digitized information erases distinctions that were driven primarily by the media in which the information was stored, not the information itself. For example, a library traditionally separates materials by media, putting newspapers in one place, audiovisual materials in another, government documents in yet another. The general collection is confined to materials printed in books.

Financial offices were among the first to operate in a totally digital environment. Most programs were developed for the efficient management of numeric data, but often depended on transferring information at some point or other into paper form. The integration of databases designed to manage numeric data and those designed to manage text provides the basis for the development of a corporate memory system. Once information is in digital form, it can be stored and retrieved electronically. Instead of storing retrieval aids, such as indexes, in one medium and the material in another, digitized information can be accessible regardless of the form in which it was originally produced.

Moreover, the retrieved information can be delivered on paper, as a fax or in electronic files. The production and management of information in digital form is media-independent.

Business needs

In order to survive, technology must meet the needs of business, not vice versa. Technology should open new opportunities for the business. Identifying the core functions of a business is necessary if a corporate memory management system is to be properly introduced. This requires the establishment of a clear line of sight from each and every business activity to the customer. Thus, the elimination of intermediaries is an essential part of workflow analysis. The corporate memory system must meet the mission of the organization: information is kept in the corporate memory because it is useful, because it meets the needs of customers or potential customers, or is of value to functions that meet customer needs. The technology will enable staff to answer customer questions directly instead of acting on a file and subsequently sending it back for more information. As the customer is enabled to access the same information that is available to the staff, the constant shuffling of paper can be eliminated.

The indexing and retrieval systems that are now available enable staff at the workgroup level to improve upon the indexing and description of information. This can be carried on in the automated environment, eliminating the cost of indexing and reindexing.

SGML and workflow

The application of SGML and its derivative technologies makes significant workflow changes. Paper documents normally enter the organization through the mail room. The use of SGML technology necessitates minimum classification and document description at the point of entry and, when possible, the digitization of documents so that they can be moved through the organization electronically. Electronic documents arriving in the organization also need to be indexed. Once this is done, document handling and reclassification tasks can often be completely eliminated.

As more and more information on the Internet uses standard markup language, the possibility of a common way to organize information is being created. These markup codes can be used whether the information is generated internally or externally. Using the standard markup language, however, also enables improved searching and access. Documents encoded using SGML can be accessed and then presented for viewing, using either browsing or search techniques. Titles may be browsed in sequence according to a particular classification scheme, then reordered by a second scheme and browsed again. Other elements can also be browsed, and a subset of document elements can be presented to assist the searcher in recognizing relevant documents. Hence, a searcher can easily search all titles, tables of contents, or illustrations. Descriptive and indexed catalogs can be created automatically and full-text or element specific searches can be performed.

SGML-encoded documents can be searched directly. Queues of documents can be created by any desired classification and selection criteria and examiners can look at, evaluate and return each document before continuing to the next.

Automating documents

The shift from data manipulation to work process improvement means that information must be organized around work processes, rather than traditional departments and structures. Responsibility and authority move to the lowest possible level. In order to use existing technology effectively, responsibility for work must be delegated to the workgroups.

In order to do this properly, workflow analysis needs to identify the business of the organization and the work necessary to meet its business needs.

Too often, automation emulates the hierarchical work process traditional in government and industry: work is organized from the top down. Mainframe technology, which dominated the early automation period, used the computer as an instrument of control, and in order to accomplish work, it was necessary to go through those who controlled the computer. Power came from the ability to control access to information and access to changes in the way information was processed.

Much of the hierarchical nature of an organization was determined by the technology of paper flow. Moving a document from place to place required a large army of middle managers to process and filter paper. As information becomes accessible in new ways, work begins to flow in new ways. Information is accessible across organizational lines. Documents are circulated in draft form and often never find their way to final 'approval'.

Current technology is based on the principle that the flow of work needs to be analyzed and that authority and responsibility needs to move to the lowest possible level. The workflow is designed to make sure that there is a clear line of sight to the customer. As the system is redesigned, new skills will be needed by the workforce. In general, as authority and responsibility are decentralized, fewer and fewer managers and supervisors are needed.

The very act of automating a process changes the way that business is done and requires, in turn, further automation. In other words, by the time an automation process is completed it is already obsolete, for the systems used to accomplish the work were based on old ways of doing business.

Electronic imaging technology enables work to be done anywhere in the world. People no longer need to live near their workplaces, or even to work in an office: they can live anywhere in the world and still be part of an electronic workgroup. This is cost-effective, for the cost of moving images is much less than the cost of moving staff. However, this only works when the technology leads to the empowerment of workers. In fact, bringing automation into work situations without re-engineering the workflow frequently leads to expensive disillusionment. As work is dispersed, communities will develop to take full advantage of the intellectual, social and cultural life that builds the kind of broadly educated staff needed to work in the electronic environment. Moreover, the need to build large buildings to house staff and paper diminishes as information is brought directly to the workplace, and workplaces can be dispersed throughout the world.[23]

Strategies for documentation

The widespread elimination of the file copy requires corporations to adopt new documentation strategies as information systems are developed. Unfortunately, many records managers and archivists rely on thought patterns developed in the paper world and outmoded concepts of documents and records. As was seen in the earlier discussion of the new document, a document in an electronic environment is a response to a query. It is a set of atomic elements held together by a meaning given by the use of the document.

However, a record is a documentation of a transaction. As part of the workflow it is necessary to identify copies of documents that need to be stored in the corporate memory and to develop a system to capture these documents at appropriate points in the workflow. In the paper world a file copy was made when a document was 'signed off' by the appropriate official. A few documents that belong in the corporate memory will be such formally approved or signed-off actions, but today the informal exchange of information that is characteristic of the electronic environment requires the development of a deliberate policy of how and when documentation is collected, and how long it will be maintained.

The computer-driven office enables rapid and repeated sharing of information. Teamwork and cooperation replace the division of labor characteristic of previous industrial production. The Rules of Worth discussed earlier should be used to decide which documents need to be captured for the corporate memory. These principles can, to a considerable extent, be built into automated systems by either making a default disposition of documents in certain offices or by specifying limited choices appropriate for each staff member.

---

[23] See Megill, Thinking for a Living.

The application of these rules will require an analysis of the activities of each workgroup, and analyzing the appropriate place for the rules in the workflow will be one of the most important tasks of the corporate memory manager. As this analysis is completed the corporate memory system can be populated as a routine part of the workflow. Staff members will need to make only a few decisions, prior to closing records, which will provide the key information on the contents of the corporate memory. By customizing these decisions for each staff member, the system will allow choices to be made with maximum uniformity while allowing the staff member initiative and creativity.

As part of the normal workflow metadata will be supplied automatically, by human intervention or a combination of both, to:

- identify the type of document (letter, memorandum, report etc.) from a list;
- identify keywords that describe the content of the document. These descriptors will come from a thesaurus or other controlled vocabulary to ensure uniformity throughout the organization. A staff member should always be free to add additional descriptors after a review by an information professional who can determine whether the controlled vocabulary needs to be modified;
- identify the value of the document:
  (a) Is it purely personal? If so, the document would not become a part of the corporate memory system. As a precaution the default would normally include a document in the corporate memory, but every staff member should be able to determine and identify a document as purely personal. Of course, if the material is shared with others it becomes a part of the corporate memory system.
  (b) If the document is not purely personal its disposition (e.g. circulation, confidentiality and retention period) needs to be determined by the answers to a few simple questions, such as:
    (1) Is the document being sent to an important office or official? The definition of important can be determined in advance, but the staff member can also be asked to identify the eventual destination of the document.
    (2) Is the document prepared in response to a request by an 'important' official?
    (3) Is the document sent to another office and, if so, which?
    (4) Is there any law or regulation that requires the document to be kept? By analyzing the workflow of the staff member, a

determination of the possible records requiring a legal retention period can be identified.

With such a system the individual staff member can determine the value of a document within a framework that ensures organization-wide consistency. This is the key to the development of a corporate memory system. When the application of the rules yields conflicting time periods, then the longer period should prevail. An exception to this rule is to destroy records for which the legal time has expired, unless there is a strong organizational need to keep the record for longer.

CHAPTER TEN

Improvements

The task of managing the corporate memory appears daunting. It is obviously impossible to bring all the available information under control at the same time. Even if we accept the importance of making the corporate memory available for reuse, it is often difficult to know where to start.

One of the major temptations of information technology is to try to solve all problems at the same time. Too often bureaucracies create information systems that meet their own needs rather than the customers' and take on a life of their own. Information systems need to be developed to meet the needs of the customers of the organization or business. Corporate memory systems need to be developed from below and be based on an analysis of information products produced in the course of doing work that have value for re-use. Identifying the work is the most important prerequisite for a successful implementation of a corporate memory system.

The work of an organization is not just what it does. It is more than the tasks that are carried out in a work place. Creating an information sharing culture requires a reward system and leadership. During this transition period to a new way of doing work, improvements can be made in work processes and the stage set for a new work culture based on information sharing. This work culture requires an effective corporate memory system to enable the work products (information packets) of value for re-use to be identified and managed.

> Workflow is the sequence of tasks, or necessary steps, that comprise a business process. To understand the workflow of an organization, it is important to look at things from a process perspective, rather than from an organizational perspective. In other words, it is not the particular office that does work . . . there are processes that often cut across organizational units. Simply laying out the bureaucratic structure of the organization will not give us the workflow.
>
> It is possible for two groups to perform the same work, but have an entirely different workflow. In other words, the way that any particular group accomplishes its work may be very different, but the work may be the same. Work is not about how you spend your time; it is about what, if anything, you accomplish.
>
> Megill, Thinking for a Living, p. 150.

Organizations need a strategy that enables them to understand the specific, concrete tasks that need to be accomplished. In sum, the development of decentralized information systems means that the age of the single big system that will solve our information problems is over.

A long-term goal

Even in good economic times no one can afford to lose information, recreate lost information, waste time hunting for it, or store obsolete, useless and redundant information on ever-increasing disk storage. The costs are too high to avoid addressing the management of corporate memory. Establishing a corporate memory system should be viewed as a long-term goal, and not as a quick automation project. Any organization can hope only to tackle the corporate memory a little at a time, using the best tools and models available to automate each part. As with any good long-term goal, however, there are many ways to reach it and with proper planning and organization, the goal is attainable.

The changes in the computing environment of the last decade have set the stage for developing systems to manage corporate memory. In order to do this, its contents must be organized, retrievable and in context by communities.

Often the most difficult part of change is beginning. There are ready-to-use automation technologies to begin managing the corporate memory.[24] The option of doing nothing – or delaying so long that nothing is done – is not viable.

Developing a corporate memory system requires a strategic plan, to be implemented over time. Before this plan is made, however, it is possible for a corporate memory manager to make individual improvements that can set the stage for a corporate memory system. The following list of improvements is adapted from those made by Carlos A. Cuadra in his paper 'The Corporate Memory and the Bottom Line', distributed by Cuadra Associates. Many of them will help an information management system be more efficient. They are not a substitute for a plan, but can demonstrate the value of improved information management.

Improvement 1: Taking inventory

Developing an inventory of an organization's information and information systems is usually valuable. The types and characteristics of information in the organization's computer systems – on local drives, network servers, disks and tapes – and on paper and microfilm reveal duplications and provide information for future system improvements.

Records managers often start with an inventory, but in practice it is seldom completed. If automation is an ongoing activity, as it is in most organizations, the inventory is quickly outdated and cannot be completed before the picture changes. Taking inventory is only the first step towards bringing information under control. An inventory is, at best, a snapshot in time. Even in a small organization, after any given disk drive is inventoried the contents will quickly change, because new documents are created daily. The corporate memory, by its very nature, is volatile and any solution to the problem of managing it must include dynamic updating. Nevertheless, making a rough inventory is a useful activity that will improve the management of any information system.

Improvement 2: Duplicating copies or index cards

Making multiple copies of each document or document representation – one per file folder or location where staff members might look for such

---

[24] When I wrote the first edition of this book I said that little progress is being made in managing corporate memory. That situation has changed with the development of several robust electronic records management systems and document management systems.

Box 10.1 Taking inventory

Nearly every records or information management text gives an example of an inventory. One of the best is available without cost from the National Archives and Records Administration in *Disposition of Federal Records*, by Richard Wire, published in 1992 and revised in 1997. An inventory lists the various types (or series) of records in an organization, how many are created each year and the volume on hand. In addition, information on format, whether the same information is contained elsewhere, and who is responsible for maintaining the collected records, should be included.

An inventory is normally the first step recommended by a records manager. In the rapidly changing environment of electronic records, however, its value is diminished. For electronic records the inventory is often done for information systems, based on the technology being used. Another, more useful, replacement for the traditional inventory is an analysis of the workflow and work processes. Understanding the work and information products are more important than inventorying items.

---

information – is a traditional way of capturing the corporate memory. In many offices the problem is solved by making duplicate photocopies and spreading them throughout the organization. Electronic file copying now makes this process easier than ever, so that wordprocessed files can be copied and easily dispersed. As everyone knows, however, control of the information is quickly lost when any attempt to determine its flow or location depends on the memory of those involved.

Improvement 3: Using shared servers

This solution involves putting electronic documents on a shared disk or server. The server system removes documents from local disks to a single shared disk and can be compared to allowing a number of people to share a desk. However, this can create problems. Information on a shared disk may not be organized in a way that allows anyone other than the originator to find it. Without a descriptive index to file contents, and without Boolean or other text-searching capabilities, finding the right information can be very difficult and time-consuming. Without a retention schedule or other systematic means of purging, the files will simply accumulate, using up disk storage and making searching increasingly difficult.

Box 10.2 Using index cards: the BBC

Until a few years ago, the News Division of the British Broadcasting Corporation employed a system that used index cards to manage its corporate memory, which was a vault filled with unique film and video footage. BBC staff members viewed and cataloged each film, describing each scene in terms of locale, participants, reporter, date, subject matter and other valuables. An index card was made for each aspect of the film and the collection of cards for each film was filed at multiple points – typically 10 to 20 – in a massive card catalog. Systems such as this work well, but they are costly and time consuming.

They can also be problematic. For example, a few years ago the resignation of a prominent Government minister five minutes before news time created extraordinary pressure for immediate location of the piece of film that was required. Fortunately, the BBC had already solved both the cost and the time problems by bringing in an automated multiuser information management system to replace the card catalog. Once installed, the required films were found within seconds.

In many organizations servers may be organized geographically (e.g. one server per floor or per department); such a system can cause serious access problems if the users who share information are located on differing floors or in separate departments. Still, sharing the storage of files, even if only in a limited area, is generally an improvement.

Improvement 4: Imaging

One proposed solution to the document-loss problem is to store everything in image (bit-mapped) format. This approach has considerable appeal, since it ensures that there is at least one copy of each document. With appropriately configured personal computers on a network, one can theoretically provide access to any and all documents from any computer. Enthusiasm for this approach can wane when one considers the cost of scanning and the amount of disk storage a single black-and-white document page requires (about 50 kilobytes, even when compressed by a factor of 20:1). In addition, considering the many kinds of documents that need to be scanned, both the cost and the required disk space are increased. Even if the cost of scanning and storing were not forbidding, this approach makes sense only if the image management system includes capabilities for locating imaged documents by means of their contents.

Much of the information that comes into the organization can be captured using electronic forms and/or automatic form readers. The development of electronic forms and the ability to capture selected information and bring it into existing databases is a traditional part of the work of the records manager. Forms mean that information comes into the organization in standard layouts and can be captured into databases that are easily manipulable. Imaging, combined with optical character recognition, enables forms to be automated. Although imaging is a powerful technology that enables documents and parts of documents to be stored in a digital, rather than a paper, form, it is only part of a solution to the problem of managing the corporate memory. In practice, it is simply another way to copy documents.

Improvement 5: PC-based file-finding software

A number of PC-based file-finding utilities address the lost-document problem. These products have a limited usefulness in managing the corporate memory, for a number of reasons:

1. Retrieval from large databases is generally slow.
2. The access points provided for retrieval are usually limited and inflexible. For example, one cannot specify that the desired item is a report received during the last 6 months of the last year, or that the expiry date for the patents on a particular competitor's biggest-selling product has passed.
3. Retrieval is limited to the disk drives on the individual PC or attached network file server.

Some organizations try to manage their corporate memory by dumping the contents of their wordprocessed documents (and the text derived from scanned hardcopy documents) into a system with full-text (only) storage and retrieval software. (David C. Blair and M.E. Marion: An Evaluation of Retrieval Effectiveness for a Full-text Document Retrieval System. Communications of the ACM, March 1985). This solution has serious drawbacks because:

1. They lack structure. Full-text databases do not allow for precise retrieval, such as through specification of date range, type of document, the creator or addresses of the document, or persons to whom copies were sent.

2. The format in which documents are stored makes reconstructing the original document impossible.
3. Full-text systems make no provision for applying a retention schedule to determine how long documents should be retained.

Getting started

In most organizations some of the steps described above are already being taken to build corporate memory systems. The initial steps have sometimes been taken by records offices, sometimes by librarians, and sometimes by management information staff who recognize the growing problem of identifying the organization's memory. In other organizations the general counsel, who is responsible for defending the organization's integrity, may be the person who recognizes the problem caused by staff turnover and loss of corporate memory.

In conclusion, such individual improvements provide some starting points for building a corporate memory system. However, they result in a fragmented system and fail to capture one or more of the elements essential for corporate memory.

CHAPTER ELEVEN

Making it happen

So we approach the end of our journey. We have looked at the need for saving corporate memory, identified its contents, learned how to evaluate its worth and mused about the problem of getting started. We have also seen that information needs to be viewed as a totality, regardless of its source. The distinction between internal and external information that has traditionally separated the library from the business activities of an organization vanishes.

By recognizing that information is information, regardless of its source, and by identifying the lessons learned by the various information professions, we create the basis for developing a corporate memory system. This is possible because the technology exists to enable us to manage large volumes of information and data electronically. The requirements of a system to manage corporate memory were enumerated, and we discussed how learning needs to take place in a technological environment.

All that is left is to start building. Below are some illustrative sequences for developing the corporate memory system. They are illustrative for they are not meant to be prescriptions on how to proceed. They are sequences for they provide a series of steps to build a corporate memory system. Each of these sequences can be part of a strategic plan. They go beyond simply improving the current systems to building an integrated corporate memory system.

What is important is that changes are made as a part of a plan that brings corporate memory under control. As information is recognized as being as asset of the company, it is seen as a product with value in itself. Vast amounts of data now exist in electronic form. When this data is made available along with other data crated elsewhere in the organization, its value may increase. From the organization's point of view capturing the data for future use should be the major criterion in establishing a corporate memory system.

The problem with electronic data is the same as with all other information – decisions need to be made on its value. Once these decisions are made, systems need to be developed to keep the information for the appropriate period of time and retrieve it when required. The integration of text retrieval and data retrieval is one of the most important aspects of the corporate memory system. In the end, all information needs to be analyzed and viewed within the context of its use by the organization. Artificial distinctions between images and paper, and between electronic data and information, are not helpful. There are a number of places to start, but a system needs to be built that will capture all of the components of the corporate memory. No matter where you start, the goal and end result are the same.

Alternative Starting Point I: People

In the past the organization has generally relied upon its staff to recall when key events occurred, why certain decisions were made or ideas discarded, how something is supposed to work and where vital information can be found. Unfortunately, the collective experience and know-how of the individuals in an organization cannot be bottled and indexed or abstracted for others to use. Nevertheless, there are many good reasons to institutionalize and manage what we can of the total set of information comprising the corporate memory.

In every organization there are people who perform the function of keeping the corporate memory. One way to start building the corporate memory is to identify these people and talk with them. Knowledge management describes this process as making explicit the tacit knowledge of an organization. Finding these people is an informal task: nowhere on the organizational chart is the corporate memory keeper identified. They are the persons you will discover when you ask 'Who do you ask if you wonder how a policy was developed or if you cannot find a document using the normal procedures or channels?' Often the keeper of the memory will be retired or nearing retirement. Sometimes it is a person who once held an important position in the organization but no longer does so. It is seldom the person or persons who have responsibility for the organization. The current decision makers seldom have the time or perspective to worry about the corporate memory. Those who do are often more than willing to talk. If you listen carefully, you will be able to identify what important documents need to be found and put into the corporate memory system.

Don't limit the search for memory keepers to high-level employees. For example, there is often a secretary or someone in a similar position who knows how to find things that are lost. These are often low-profile employees, but once identified they can be extremely valuable in building the corporate memory. As these people are identified, ask who they consult when they need to find out something. Your search will quickly yield a network of people, which will cut across organizational lines.

Often these people have stature within the organization and they also probably understand intuitively what you are trying to do, so talking to them will build a political base for the introduction of a corporate memory system. As you talk with them, identify what documents they have in their possession and arrange to get copies of them for the corporate memory, if possible.

Once the keepers of corporate memory are identified, call them together and organize a team to document activities or events. The committee need not meet often, but it can support you as you build the corporate memory and can give advice on the best way to bring the key documents into the system. Particularly troublesome requests for information can often be referred to one or more members of this team. By using the keepers of the memory to build the automated system, you will greatly enrich the quality of information in the system.

The process of documentation is, as we have seen, not just collecting the residue of an organization's activity. A strategy is needed to identify how to document the organization's activities. The memory keepers may not be technology friendly and may even be opposed to its introduction. They know better than anyone how badly technology can damage or destroy components of the corporate memory, or they have often lived through such experiences. You need to bear in mind that you are building an automated system to replace the informal system: you must respect and be sensitive to their views and needs.

As you work with the people who keep the memory, you will identify documents that need to be described and scanned into the corporate memory system. By indexing these documents and making them a part of the system, you will link them to documents currently being produced. The key documents from the past can provide real help to staff members as they begin to use the corporate memory system.

Alternative Starting Point II: Electronic data

Another place to start is to identify existing electronic data that can become part of the corporate memory. Many organizations already are adopting the concept of warehousing data. The term is perhaps misleading, for it sees data as being stored away waiting for someone to ask for it, rather than as an important resource at hand.

If there is a data warehousing program, it is one logical place to begin building a corporate memory system. In order to make the data valuable, they need to be linked to other information sources and made accessible through modern search engines. The principle value of a corporate memory system is to make information available for reuse by staff that did not create it and may not even know that it exists.

Often an organization's data resides in relational databases accessed in the routine performance of a business activity. Data management systems are generally operated to use and manipulate data in a particular context. The corporate memory system needs to incorporate these data, but it will need to see the information as having a value beyond the context in which it was created and typically used.

One of the advantages of beginning with electronic data is that data managers generally exercise some level of control over the databases, and generally have procedures to ensure the integrity of the data in the system. Databases are routinely and regularly backed up. Copies of data are often taken to an off-site storage area for protection against fire or other disasters, and duplicates are kept in case of hardware or software failure.

Alternative Starting Point III: Electronic documents

All of these processes are essential for the successful operation of electronic data systems, but are not sufficient for a corporate memory system. A backup does not enable us to retrieve information quickly and easily because a backup system is developed primarily to protect against system failures.

The backup system provides us with one starting point for developing the corporate memory system. What is needed is to develop procedures to evaluate the data from the viewpoint of the organization as a whole, and determine what needs to be kept for reuse.

Data in an organization is in flux, with a multitude of users adding, deleting and editing. Much is of transitory value and need not be preserved beyond the short-term needs of the business. It is normally not necessary, nor feasible, to save all data and all changes in the data systems for later use. The increasing amounts of information in electronic data systems require us to decide what is needed from the warehousing program for the corporate memory system. We need to determine the value of the data – who uses it, when, and how often.

This strategy may be particularly valuable when the organization regularly uses databases in its work but does not have a way to save its historical memory. Many database systems do not provide historical information without considerable difficulty. This is particularly true where the organization has gone through various generations of computers, and not all information has been migrated each time. In other situations, information is stored on disks that are not readily available online.

If the organization is undertaking a data warehousing program this will provide one place to begin. The advantage of starting here is that the databases are often maintained centrally. The power of the corporate memory will only become apparent, however, when the information in the databases can be integrated with the information being generated in wordprocessed documents.

Electronic documents include wordprocessed documents, e-mail and scanned images. They also can include records/transcripts of instant messaging systems and other collaborative tools. Documents are information packets held together because they are used together. The elements of an electronic document may not all be physically stored together, but the linkages from one element to another and the relationships created by these linkages create a document. Documents are kept as informational packets and normally need to be accessed as such. They may include not just the text, but also other information such as formatting instructions in wordprocessed documents and, for e-mail, the history of the delivery of the document.

Unlike data, documents are kept together because they have meaning. They are organized data held together by use. They may be stored in various elements, and may exist as a compound document. Unlike data in a company-wide system, the storage of electronic documents is not normally centralized. In order to manage electronic documents it is necessary to identify documents dispersed on personal computers and networks that should be part of the corporate memory system.

In many organizations the library or technical information center manages information obtained externally. The records management unit manages information generated by or used by the organization. The management information systems or information technology groups manage information stored in electronic form. But in most organizations no-one is assigned to manage the wordprocessed files – the correspondence, memos and other documents created by the employees – although such documents represent a growing majority of information in an organization.

Neither library automation nor records management systems are designed to deal with the mass of wordprocessed documents being produced within organizations: they cannot capture and process the source information at the time the document is crated. What is needed is a system that supports the easy capture, automatic indexing, easy retrieval and planned retirement or destruction of documents.

Most wordprocessed files exist for a time in both paper and electronic form. Version control is essential for the proper management of wordprocessed files. So, too, is information about who the document is from and to, as well as who has copies of it and what modifications may have been made. In the age of electronic manipulation the way in which the document develops and how it is used can be important. Because the native wordprocessed formats may have links to other files and may be needed again in the same format, the location of the native(original) file on the PC network disk is also necessary, in order to have an adequate corporate memory database. The user searches the corporate memory database to find the appropriate documents and, if the original file is needed – either for reference or to be incorporated into another work product – it can be displayed.

The potential benefits of managing documents from cradle to grave are numerous. Users can find the right file quickly – not just their own but, more importantly, those created by others. They can use them to create new versions or as departure points for creating new but similar documents, building on previous work and thereby saving considerable time and effort. The advantage of starting with wordprocessed documents is that such files can often be identified and retrieved directly from the network. In order to bring these documents within the corporate memory, however, it will be necessary to identify a special place (normally a server devoted exclusively to housing the corporate memory) on the network to collect them.

In order to incorporate wordprocessed files into the corporate memory, the staff will need to make some basic decisions about documents.

1. What is the worth of the document? In an earlier chapter we discussed the ways and means to determine the worth of documents using the traditional criteria of archivists and records managers. In the end, judg-

ment must be applied by someone who is both knowledgeable and trained. Staff members may be knowledgeable but not trained, and the corporate memory system should enable the appropriate staff member to make decisions in a prescribed context. Normally, any given staff member will handle documents that have only two or three different dispositions. For example, they can identify whether a document is purely personal and should not go to the corporate memory system. Making this decision will protect the privacy of the individual's work. It will also mean that the document cannot be shared with others and remains the total responsibility of the individual. Work that is not purely personal would normally be one of two different dispositions – perhaps a long or a short retention period. The decision about which documents fall into which category can best be made by their creator. Of course, the decision can be changed by someone else in the organization, who may recognize value in the document that the creator does not see.

2. What kind of document is it e.g. letter, memo, or report? This decision is generally obvious to the staff member working on the document, but it is often very difficult for others to determine at a later time. For a particular staff member there may be specialized document types that need to be identified, such as forms or specific reports.

3. What is the document about? One lesson learned from online searching is that descriptors which tell us what the document is about greatly increased effective retrieval. Full-text searching, by itself, is often not sufficient to find many desired documents, but a document can often be retrieved by author, date or similar information that can be automatically captured by the corporate memory system. It is important, however, for someone to identify the subject of the document. This is best done by selecting from a list of subjects that are appropriate for the office. The opportunity to specify additional subjects should be given, and these should be collected and reviewed by the records manager to determine if they should be added to the thesaurus or list of subjects. These subjects can be used as a controlled vocabulary for database searching purposes and greatly increase the retrievability of records.

In order for the staff to make these decisions, you will need to develop the following:

1. A thesaurus that functions as a controlled vocabulary for the organization. Building a thesaurus is an ongoing activity. It begins by identifying some of the key terms that need to be applied to wordprocessed documents.

2. A list of document types used in the organization. Reports, memos and letters are normal, and other specialized reports should be identified.
3. A retention schedule. If one already exists it needs to be evaluated for its usefulness with electronic documents. It is important that the same retention apply to all documents of the same type and containing the same kind of information, regardless of the medium on which they are kept. Most retention schedules were developed with the assumption that information is primarily kept in paper form. We know, however, that 85% of the information in an organization is now in wordprocessed files. The primary record is not electronic.

Each of these requires management support to make decisions that are often difficult. However, one or more parts of the organization may be pilots for managing wordprocessed documents electronically, but the corporate memory system will not be in place until all wordprocessed files are captured.

Managing wordprocessed fields is not as straightforward as it might appear, and defining a technically achievable and user-acceptable system is challenging. The specific requirements for any system will of course vary depending upon the nature and needs of the organization. The following list gives an indication of the possible kind of requirements for managing wordprocessed documents.

1. Staff members who file the documents should be able to use their current wordprocessing software, without having to change packages.
2. Those who create wordprocessed documents should be the ones to decide which to file in the corporate memory, on the basis of guidance from the organization.
3. The system should not require special document collectors or indexers. (If it did, processing of the documents could be delayed and the documents would effectively be lost until they were processed.)
4. Even though all words in the document would be automatically indexed, the document creators should contribute value-added descriptions to each. This provides for better and more precise retrieval because most of the added indexing can be done by the document creators themselves.
5. In addition to prompting for specific information the system should capture default data, such as the name and release number of the wordprocessing software used, the date and the document creator and office. Such information is already known to the wordprocessing software and should never need to be entered again.

6. There must be provisions for passwording and maintaining the security of the data in the corporate memory. Only those persons authorized to see particular parts of it should have access to those parts.
7. The corporate memory system must incorporate basic tools of records management so that electronic records are maintained on a schedule. The records should be kept for as long as is legally required but not long enough to become a legal liability.
8. The system must include version control. For example, forms and policy and procedure documents are often revised over a period of time. In some instances staff members may need to trace the history of a particular procedure, reviewing all of the versions. In other cases only the most current version is wanted. A corporate memory system must meet both these requirements, allowing for an audit of all of the versions while making it easy to find the current version.
9. The system should provide for linking content-based retrieval with immediate access to the corporate memory copy in the native word-processing format, so that users can print or modify the retrieved document or create a new document.
10. The system should not require any desirable procedures already in place to be abandoned.
11. The system should have built-in capabilities for handling four-digit years, for easy transition to next-century dates with no programming or other system modification.
12. There should be a procedure to ensure that file names are used consistently.

Alternative Starting Point IV: What comes in the door

A fourth possible place to begin to develop the corporate memory system is to focus on information as it comes into the organization. By capturing information at the point of entry, it can be brought under control prior to its dispersal in the organization. Incoming information may be in electronic or paper form. If it is on paper it should be digitized immediately; the paper can then be stored away with a relatively short retention period and the electronic version can be distributed throughout the organization. The development of imaging technology makes this possible. The initial indexing at the point of entry is one of the most important activities in the entire process. It will require a shift of function on the part of some mailroom personnel, from being fetchers and haulers to being information specialists. Talented and well-educated staff at the point of entry into the information system is one of the most important requirements for a corporate memory management system. As the mailroom becomes the information processing center, staff will be able to work cooperatively in real time and call upon colleagues for assistance in real time. There may be little reason for staff to go to the office every day; work may be done when, where and how they choose.

By starting with information as it comes into the organization, it is possible to start afresh. Information from older systems can be digitized as it is needed. It is not necessary, therefore, to digitize all existing information to develop a corporate memory system.

The technology for managing images developed in the insurance and other industries, where there were large numbers of forms needed to be routed through the organization. Imaging the documents as they arrived offered obvious advantages, since they immediately became available to all those who needed them. The technology is now mature enough to be of use in nearly any organization.

Differing scenarios

Each of these scenarios need not take place in isolation, and parts of each will be needed in order to build a complete system. How and where to start is a practical and political decision. No situation is ideal and none will enable full and complete immediate implementation of the corporate memory system.

Regardless of the strategy used, as the system is built and developed clear advantages to the work of the organization needs to be shown as quickly as possible. It is also important that the normal workflow be interrupted as little as possible during the implementation process. The savings in time and space that will emerge will be great and, if the implementation is done properly, it will be paid for by these savings. Using existing systems and implementing the corporate memory system when and where it can most easily be done will bring immediate successes and improvements. It is important, however, that there should be a strategy and implementation plan that leads to the creation of a totally integrated corporate memory system, allowing all staff access to it using simple search tools tailored to meet their needs.

One of the major problems with any new system is that of converting old information – much of the corporate memory may not even be documented, and when it is it is often not widely available to the organization.

One way to start is to choose a certain day and begin to collect information, perhaps in a particular part of the organization. Don't worry about the past, just about capturing what arrives in the future or what is used in the future.

The chief indication of what may be appropriate for use in the future is what is used now. As information is identified for which there is a serious need, it can be brought into the corporate memory.

Most information in an office has a life span of a month. After that time, information is reused for about 3 months and then reuse drops off dramatically. After another 3 years there is another drop in use. Therefore, from the viewpoint of day-to-day operations a corporate memory system can be installed over a period of a year without worrying about converting the entire contents of the legacy systems.

A Knowledge Application Service

Much of what has been written here assumes that a corporate memory system will be developed by in-house staff. This need not be the case. Why would a company, organization or agency have an in-house corporate memory manager? Do they have an in-house Certified Public Accountant or General Counsel? Even if they do, they hire outside professionals to ensure the professional competency of their work.

Outsourcing business processes takes the concept of service bureaus and application service providers to its next step. Traditional service bureaus deliver particular services, such as imaging, data capture, or other activities. Application Service Providers manage software remotely and make it available to customers.

An application is a set of business processes. Managing corporate memory is a logical business application – the business processes described in this book. The Corporate Memory Application goes beyond the traditional service bureau, for it provides the full range of professional records management services to an organization.

A knowledge application service may provide professional corporate memory services that may be provided by an in-house corporate memory manager. These might include, but not be limited to, representing the organization to governmental bodies as needed.

In order for customers to take advantage of the Corporate Memory Application, they commit themselves to doing their work in an integrated digital environment – an environment in which information is made immediately available to those who need it for their work.

Using the corporate memory

In the end, the effort of creating a corporate memory system is in vain unless the information is used. Documents containing information that may be reused are prime candidates to enter the system. Tracking who uses which documents and for what purposes is one of the most important parts of the work of the corporate memory manager. It goes beyond just reporting to the bureaucracy, but provides hints of new and inventive ways in which information can be recycled and reused.

As staff begin to use the corporate memory, they will continue to learn about the system. It will be important to advertise ways in which the information contained in the corporate memory can save time and effort, so that its full power can be used. Learning is an ongoing process and building the learning organization will be facilitated by the development of the corporate memory system. As staff become comfortable with the fact that they no longer need to keep their own personal copies, and can learn from the work done by others, they will understand the power of this. The technology will develop and new uses for the information will increase.

Staff will begin to see the full value of the work they do, and to see their work as part of the work of the entire organization, and not just of their department. A sense of pride and context may well be one of the most important results of a corporate memory system. This sense of place enables individuals to see that their work is important as part of the organization, and not just to a particular person at a particular time.

In building the corporate memory system, if you have a goal you can start almost anywhere and end up at the right place.

For Further Information

Asprey, Len and Middleton, Michael. *Integrative Document and Content Management: Strategies for Exploiting Enterprise Knowledge.* Hershey, PA: Idea Group. 2003.

Written from the viewpoint of document management, this hefty volume provides guidance for selecting automated document management systems.

Bearman, David. *Electronic Evidence: Strategies for Managing Records in Contemporary Organizations.* Pittsburgh: Archives and Museum Infomatics, 1994.

A collection of articles written by a theorist working on the issue of managing electronic records. He concentrates on managing electronic information and ensuring that data become actual records. To do this, the context and structure, as well as the content, of the data must be maintained. Bearman also discusses the need for standards in the documentation of electronic records.

'Bench Marking, Total Quality Management, the Learning Organization. New Management Paradigms for the Information Environment,' Special Libraries. 84(3), 1993, 120–157.

A special issue that includes the importance of developing a 'learning organization' and its relationship to the information professions. This publication by the Special Libraries Association includes a useful bibliography.

Bentley, Trevor, J. *Making Information Systems Work For You.* Englewood Cliffs, NJ: Prentice-Hall, 1983.

As an accountant, manager and systems designer, the author discusses practical ideas to avoid the problems that inevitably occur between information provider and user. He focuses on human factors such as management style and reaction to change. There is particular emphasis on the need to understand information requirements from the perspective of both manager and user prior to beginning the system design. He offers detailed advice and plans for each aspect of the system lifecycle. The information remains relevant today for business managers, information professionals and students, since the system concepts detailed reflect the network and open systems ideas appropriate for current technology.

The Commission on Preservation and Access and The Research Libraries Group. 'Preserving Digital Information,' Report of the Task Force on Archiving of Digital Information. Washington DC 1996

Although this report deals primarily with the broader question of how archived information can be preserved in the digital age, it provides many practical considerations for corporate archives. The study recommends the development of certified archives that follow mutually agreed standards, so that archived information can be preserved and shared.

The Conference Board Inc. *Information Technology: Some Critical Implications for Decision Makers.* New York: The Conference Board Inc., 1972.

This amazing report examines how technology alters the way information can (and will) be used. Information management is a prerequisite to the organization and allocation of other resources: it should focus on information itself, not on technology. The report provides an overview of information technology and its likely implications for individuals, businesses, education, libraries and government. Glaser's essay 'Information: Power without Design, Thrust without Direction' is seminal in identifying the need for policy; seeing the importance of 'new distributions in time and space of business, educational, and entertainment enterprises'; realizing that because information technology requires the development of systems as well as products, 'it might take more time to make the results acceptable to the user'; and stressing that freedom of and access to information must underlie policy choices.

Cortese, Amu. 'Here Comes the Intranet,' *Business Week.* February 26, 1996, 76–84.

This special report shows how a number of companies are using the tools designed for the Internet to manage information for internal purposes. The prediction is that intranets will quickly dwarf internets for business purposes.

Cox, Richard J. *Closing an Era. Historical Perspectives on Modern Archives and Records Management.* Westport, CT: Greenwood Press. 2000.

An archivist 's view of records management. Includes interesting historical information of the development of the archival profession as it relates to records management.

Cox, Richard J. *The First Generation of Electronic Records Archivists in the United States.* A Study in Professionalization. New York: Haworth, 1994.

An interesting discussion of the development of the archive profession, with particular emphasis on the impact of electronic records. Cox has an 'activist' view of the role of the archivist and sees this as the leader of records management.

Cox, Richard J. and Wallace, David A.(ed) *Archives and the Public Good: Accountability and Records in Modern Society.* Westport, CT: Quorum Books. 2002.

A collection of case studies on records management, most of which are reports of various failures to create and maintain accurate and reliable evidence.

Cox, Richard J. *Managing Institutional Archives: Foundational Principles and Practices.* New York: Greenwood Press. 1992.

A good textbook on the traditional way to organize and manage an institutional archive. Many of the same principles and methodologies apply to corporate contexts.

Cox, Richard J. *Managing Records as Evidence and Information.* Westport, CT: Quorum Books. 2001.

A solid discussion of the nature of records from the viewpoint of an archivist.

Cronin, Blaise and Davenport, Elisabeth. *Elements of Information Management.* Metuchen, NJ: Scarecrow Press, 1991.

This book claims that information management goes beyond formalism and rigid measurement. The models, metaphors and the associated methodologies are intended to illuminate an individual's feel for what is happening, to develop a sense of context which admits a realistic appraisal of opportunities and choices. The authors also added techniques and technologies which will help the reader to exploit the idea of total information.

Dollar, Charles M. 'Archivists and Records Managers in the Information Age.' Archivaria. (36) 1993, pp. 37–52.

Dollar was formerly a staff member at the National Archives and Records Administration of the United States federal government, where he provided leadership for improving archive and records management practices.

Dollar, Charles M. *Archival Theory and Information Technologies: The Impact of Information Technologies on Archival Principles and Methods.* Macereta, Ital: University of Macerata. 1992.

A useful overview of the basic principles of information technology by the Director of the Oxford Institute of Information Management. The book is in the Business Information Technology Series, which focuses on management issues.

Perhaps the very best and most thoughtful single book on technology and its impact on archives. It is short, succinct and on point.

Dollar, Charles M. *Authentic Electronic Records: Strategies for Long-Term Access.* Chicago: Cohassett Associations. 1999.

A practical collection of facts and advice published by a leading consulting firm in records management.

Dordick, Herbert S. and Wang, Georgette. *The Information Society: a Retrospective View.* Newbury Park, CA: Sage Publications, 1993.

An excellent discussion of the development of the information society from an international perspective. Although there is no discussion of ways in which organizations can maintain their corporate memory in the information age, this book sketches out the background against which this discussion takes place.

Earl, Michael J. *Management Strategies for Information Technology.* New York: Prentice Hall, 1989.

A useful overview of the basic principles of information technology by the Director of the Oxford Institute of Information Management. The book is in the Business Information Technology Series, which focuses on management issues.

Earl, Michael. (ed) *Information Management: The Organization Dimension.* Oxford: Oxford University. 1996.

A collection of essays on information technology's relationship to organizations. Although there is no mention of corporate memory or records management, many of the issues discussed in this book are treated by the authors.

Kerr, James and Hunter, Richard. *Inside RAD: How to Build Fully Functional Computer Systems in 90 Days or Less.* New York: McGraw-Hill, 1994.

RAD means 'rapid application development', and this presentation of one such project gives much assistance with making fast change rapidly. Kerr is one of the founders of the Information Resources Management movement. This book is valuable for someone looking to improve their workplace.

Kerr, James M. *The IRM Imperative: Strategies for Managing Information Resources.* New York: John Wiley & Sons, 1991.

This book is an impassioned plea for information systems staff to 'move out of the back room into the board room'. It gives a useful overview of integrating information management. The first two chapters discuss information resources management and the changes that are occurring. The main objective is to address the changes within an organization's foundation that must be made to make the transition from 'data management to information leverage', as well as providing the techniques and strategies to make those changes. The book is well written and provides a very useful feature – summaries and key points at the end of each chapter – for quick reference.

Lotze, Evie. *Work Culture Transformation. From Straw to Gold. The Modern Hero's Journey.* Munich: K. G. Saur, 2004.

A psychologist applies her sharp eye and years of work as a clinical psychologist using psycho drama techniques to the problem of transforming a work culture in an institution.

Maguire, Carmel, Kazlauskas, Edward J. and Weir, Anthony D. *Information Services for Innovative Organizations.* San Diego: Academic Press, 1994.

Of particular interest is the section on 'Harnessing Information Technology for Use' (5.4, pp 235–248). The authors conclude that 'Training begun early and conducted as a genuine form of information exchange can be an excellent method to lessen at least those problems likely to impede the flow of first-level efficiency effects to the organization. . . . It has been widely recognized that organizations best realize benefits from new technology when they make complementary changes in organization and management' (p. 241).

McDonald, John. 'Archives and Cooperation in the Information Age.' Archivaria. (35) 1993 pp. 110–118.

The development of electronic information sets the stage for the archivist to become an important player in information management. McDonald speaks from his experience in the Canadian archives.

McDonald, John. 'Managing Records in the Modern Office: Taming the Wild Frontier,' Archivaria (39) 1995, pp. 70–79.

One of many articles by a leader in the Canadian archives world. This article argues for the importance of bringing the records manager and the archivist into the office.

McKemmish, Sue and Upward, Frank (eds). Archival Documents. *Providing Accountability through Record Keeping.* Melbourne: Ancora Press, 1993.

The most advanced discussion on how properly to document corporate memory is taking place in Australia and Canada. This volume brings together the leading theoreticians and practitioners to consider the importance of record keeping in the electronic age. The discussion is from the viewpoint of archivists, but the proposals on strategies for documentation are of interest to all information professionals.

Megill, Kenneth A. and Herbert F. Schantz. *Document Management New Technologies for the Information Services Manager.* Munich: K. G. Saur. 1999.

Schantz is a leader in the technologies used to manage large volumes of documents and is one of the inventors of optical character recognition.

Megill, Kenneth A., Cummins, Rose, Horan, Tom, Kadec, Sarah, McLennan, Marilyn, McReynolds, Michael and Woods, Robert. *Making the Information Revolution. A Handbook for Federal Information Resources Management.* Silver Spring, MD: Association of Information and Image Management, 1995.

A cooperative work by six professionals from various information backgrounds who have worked to manage information as a resource in the national government of the United States.

Megill, Kenneth A. *Thinking for a Living. The Coming Age of Knowledge Work.* Munich: K. G. Saur, 2004.

A development of many of the ideas in this book . . . especially relating to knowledge management.

Merz, Nancy M. 'Archives and the One World of Records.' Inform. vol. 2, no. 4, April 1988, pp. 30–36.

A good explanation of why archivists and records managers should not be so separate, especially with respect to electronic records. Addresses the issue of archivists being involved with managing records from their creation, not just when they are ready to be 'reborn' in the archives.

Meyer, Christopher and Davis, Stanley M. *It's Alive: The Coming Convergence of Information, Biology, and Business.* New York: Crown Business. 2003.

The book is about change. It skillfully applies concepts taken from biology to four case studies of what they call an "adaptive enterprise."

Nelson, Michael. 'Records in the Modern Workplace: Management Concerns,' Archivaria. 39, Spring 95, pp. 80–87.

Examines threats to archives and records management from the changing nature of work, the workplace and work media, e.g. the use of portable computers, sharing of computers, e-mail systems, the increased number of entry points for information in an office and the long-term unreliability of electronic media. Concludes that 'Information principles need to be built into the hardware and software used in the office and on the road . . . These principles can be created only if the fragmentation between competing information disciplines ends'.

Penn, Ira A., Pennix, Gail and Coulson, Jim. *Records Management Handbook., 2nd edition.* Brookfield, VT: Gower, 1994.

A guide to traditional records management practices designed for the practitioner. Automation is primarily understood as automating the tracking or records, although there is recognition of developing technologies in records management.

Peters, Tom. *Liberation Management: Necessary Disorganization for the Nanosecond Nineties.* New York: Alfred A. Knopf, 1992.

This often anecdotal account offers gems that put technology development into perspective. Its strength is stimulating new ways of thinking about old problems.

The Records and Retrieval Report. *The Newsletter for Professional Information Managers.* Westport, CT: Greenwood Publishing Group.

A newsletter, published ten times a year, devoted to topics relating to records management, including the cost of producing documents.

Rifkin, Glenn. 'The Future of the Document', Forbes. October 9, 1995, pp 42–57.

Traces the move away from the paper document to the 'new document in the business world'.

Robek, Mary F., Brown, Gerald F., Stephens, David O. *Information and Records Management: Document-Based Information Systems.* New York: Glencoe/McGraw-Hill (Fourth Edition) 1995.

The most widely used textbook on records and information management describes the traditional view of records managers as the managers of the 'lowest level of filing' – the paper document.

St. Clair, Guy. *Beyond Degrees: Professional Learning for Knowledge Services.* Munich: K. G. Saur. 2003.

A challenging argument for the transformation of information services (libraries and records management) into what he calls Knowledge Services.

St. Clair, Guy. *Power and Influence: Enhancing Information Services Within the Organization.* London: Bowker-Saur, 1994.

A discussion of how information professionals can increase their influence within an organization.

St. Clair, Guy and Williamson, Joan. *Managing the New One-Person Library.* London: Bowker-Saur, 1992.

This is an updated version of the classic 1986 book that defines the role of the 'one-man band' in the information setting in an organization. Although it focuses on the one-person library, the broad range of skills required in such a setting are typical for the corporate memory manager.

Sampson, Karen. *Value-Added Records Management: Protecting Corporate Assets, Reducing Business Risks.* Westport, CT: Quorum Books. Second edition 2002

The emphasis is on vital records that are essential for the operation of a business. A sometimes plodding discussion, it does cover all one needs to know about this particular kind of record.

Schwartz, Candy and Herndon, Peter. *Records Management and the Library: Issues and Practices.* Norwood, NJ: Ablex Publishing, 1993.

A readable textbook designed to introduce records management to students in schools of library and information science.

Schwartz, Candy. *Sorting out the Web: Approaches to Subject Access.* Westport, CT: Ablex. 2001.

A readable and helpful examination by a librarian on how to "organize" the web. This is a good source for those wanting to learn more about metadata, search engines and how traditional ways to classify and organize information apply to electronic information on the Internet.

Schweitzer, James. A. *Managing Information Security: Administrative, Electronic, and Legal Measures to Protect Business Information.* Boston: Butterworths, 1990.

A useful guide to how and when an organization can protect its information. As the corporate memory system is developed, information becomes available to a much greater audience. Care is needed to ensure that information is available only to properly authorized persons.

Senge, Peter M. *The Fifth Discipline: the Art and Practice of the Learning Organization.* New York: Doubleday, 1990.

The classic book develops on learning organization. The book goes far beyond its title, proposing a 'macro theory' for information. The underlying framework of the theory is that capitalism and industrialization are the primary forces shaping the information society.' (p. 211). It is not necessary to embrace the theory to get a great deal from this stimulating book, which pulls together a number of threads that show the idea of information as a 'thing' that can be managed.

Stielow, Fred. 'Archival Theory and the Preservation of Electronic Media: Opportunities and Standards Below the Cutting Edge'. American Archivist. 55(1002) pp. 332–343.

Uses traditional archival concepts to discuss the management of electronic age. 'Preservation in this new age must respond from good management and not from a focus on conservation repairs.' (p. 343).

Stielow, Fred. *Building Digital Archives, Descriptions, and Displays: A How-go-do-it Manual for Archivists and Librarians.* New York: Neal-Schuman Publishers. 2003.

Stielow brings practical experience as a working archivist, knowledge of technology and a through grounding in the theory and practice of the information services professions to this useful manual.

Strassman, Paul A. *The Politics of Information Management: Policy Guidelines.* New Canaan, CT: Information Economics Press, 1995.

An entertaining and thought-provoking treatise by someone with experience in both corporate and government information management. Strassman looks at how information is organized and managed from the viewpoint of the manager, but with a clear understanding of the technology.

Strassman, Paul A. *The Business Value of Computers: An Executive's Guide.* New Canaan, CT: Information Economics Press, 1990.

'There is no relationship between expenses for computers and business profitability. This book shows why. You will find that similar computer technologies can lead either to monumental successes or to dismal failures.' The opening words of the introduction to this creative and stimulating book capture the position of this leader in private and public- sector technology innovation. Without a doubt, Strassman is a gifted thinker, a creative writer and a controversial business executive. Anyone looking to make improvements in an organization can profit by reading his works.

Veryard, Richard. *Information Coordination: the Management of Information Models, Systems and Organizations.* New York: Prentice Hall 1994.

'This book is about coordination at three levels: the enterprise or organization, the computerized information systems that support the enterprise and (in between) the information models of the enterprise' (p. 1). It provides useful suggestions on how to coordinate information to improve the operations of the organization. It looks at the opportunities for developing information systems that respond to the business needs of the 1990s, in contrast to the 1970s central systems with hierarchical control. The author's intent is to offer practical guidelines for developing information management systems based on current research, and by including examples of what can go wrong and why. The author presents a practical approach to developing and managing information systems and is worth reading for both business managers and information professionals.

Veryard, Richard. *Pragmatic Data Analysis.* Oxford: Blackwell Scientific Publications, 1984.

A nice little introduction to data management. Corporate memory managers should have at least some acquaintance with the basic concepts of data management, since data are the blocks from which information is built.

Weaver, Barbara N. and Bishop, Wiley L. *The Corporate Memory. A Profitable and Practical Approach to Information Management and Retention Systems,* New York: John Wiley and Sons, 1974.

Written from the point of view of a corporation, this book gives the traditional records management solutions to managing the memory of an organization. It recognizes that management information systems and records management are both concerned with the same issue: managing information. Corporate memory is defined as 'the total in-house information systems and services of an organization, which are established to collect, organize, and store efficiently all documentation generated within or coming into the company and which have the inherent feature of retrieving documents and/or information on a current and retrospective basis upon demand. Collectively, then, all record centers and data processing systems within an organization constitute the corporate memory of that organization.' (pp. 1–2). A library, for these authors, is just one more type of record center. The emphasis is on storing and maintaining centralized records repositories.

Wire, Richard A. *Disposition of Federal Records – a Records Management Handbook.* Washington, DC: National Archives and Records Administration, Office of Records Administration, 1997.

A comprehensive book for government agencies covering identification, records inventories, disposition sc hedules, their production and evaluation. It useful to any organization seeking to establish a program to manage records. Also available at www.nara.gov.

Appendix: ISO Standard

The adoption of ISO Standard 15489 in 2001 was one of the most important events in the history of records and information management. Anyone interested in developing a corporate memory system should become familiar with the standard.

I have up-dated the glossary when the standard gives a definition of a term.

The standard has two parts. Part 1 has eleven sections:

1. Scope, which makes it clear that the standard applies to all kinds of organizations and does not include the management of archival records within archival institutions.
2. Normative references which refer to related standards.
3. Terms and definitions, some of which are included in the glossary.
4. Benefits of Records Management.
5. Regulatory Environment.
6. Policy and Responsibilities.
7. Records management requirements(authenticity, reliability, integrity, and usability).
8. Design and implementation of a records system.
9. Records management processes and controls, which includes determining documents to be captured into a records system, determining how long to retain them, records capture, classification, storage and handling, access, tracking and implementing disposition.

10. Monitoring and auditing.
11. Training.

Part 2 is a technical report which gives guidelines for implementing the standard.

Glossary

Case files: A type of file traditionally used in paper filing systems. A case has an opening and closing date. Personnel files, project files, and legal case files are examples.

Corporate memory: All active and historical information in an organization that is worth sharing, managing, and preserving for re-use.

Data: Data are the "facts" or raw material that make up information.

Data management: The comprehensive management of an organization's data. Data administrators develop consistent definitions of data elements and coordinate the development of data dictionaries.

Destruction: "Process of eliminating or deleting records, beyond any possible reconstruction." ISO 15489 3.8

Disposition: "Range of processes associated with implementing records retention, destruction or transfer decisions which are documented in disposition authorities or other instruments." ISO 15489 3.9

Document: In a paper based records management system, a document is usually defined as the smallest unit for filing. It can also refer to other non-paper based articles such as computer files.

Document, noun: "Recorded information or object which can be treated as a unit." ISO 15489 3.10

Information: Information is processed data – it is the building blocks used by people when they create knowledge. Information generally requires data to be managed and processed – just as knowledge requires information to be managed and processed. But managing data and information are not identical.

Information management: The administration, use, and transmission of information and the application of theories and techniques to create, modify or improve information handling systems.

Information Resources Management (IRM): The planning, budgeting organizing, directing, training and controlling associated with the Management (IRM): creation, maintenance and use and disposition of information as well as related resources or assets such as personnel, equipment, funds, and technology. Includes data processing, telecommunications, and records management. Sometimes called Information Technology (IT).

Information System: The organized collection, processing, transmission and dissemination of information in accordance with defined procedures, whether automated or manual.

Information Technology (IT): Another term for Information Resources Management (IRM).

Inverted index: Inverted index systems are used to create an alphanumeric index of searchable terms as data are entered. Inverted indexes are traditionally used in data base management systems that manage large amounts of texts.

Knowledge: The traditional philosophical definition of knowledge is that it is justified true belief. Davenport and Prusak, two developers of knowledge management define it as "A fluid mix of framed experience values, contextual information and expert insight that provides a framework for evaluating and incorporating new experiences and information." Davenport, Thomas H. and Lawrence Prusak, Working Knowledge (Boston Harvard Business School Press, 1998) p. 5.

Knowledge Management: A methodology for making comprehensive, relevant information (current or historical) available in a timely manner for users (knowledge works) to make timely valid decisions that increase the productivity of a business application (where a business application is a set of work processes).

Life cycle of Information: The concept that information passes through: stages: creation, maintenance and use, and disposition.

Media: The physical material on which information is stored, such as paper, magnetic tape, optical disk and microform.

Metadata: "Data describing context, content and structure of records and their management through time." ISO 15489 3.12

On-line service Providers: Commercial firms that provide electronic access providers: to information of many types: weather forecasts, economic statistics, stock quotes, travel schedules, and bibliographic information, etc.

Records: "Information created, received, and maintained as evidence and information by an organization or person, in pursuance of legal obligations or in the transaction of business." ISO 15489 3.15

Records management: "Field of management responsible for the efficient and systematic control of the creation, receipt, maintenance, use and disposition of records, including processes for capturing and maintaining evidence of and information about business activities and transactions in the form of records." ISO 15489 3.16.

Registration: "Act of giving a record a unique identifier on its entry into a system." ISO 154839 3.18

Registry system: A way of keeping records widely used outside the United States to manage records. The registry system is based on records being listed in an index, often in a bound volume that serves as an index to the documents stored in a central file room.

Relational database: A type of database which is organized so that data, which is kept in a tabular format, can be accessed via queries.

Retention schedule: A list of record types and their disposition in an organization or part of an organization. Also called a disposition schedule. Making a retention (disposition) schedule is a traditional activity of records management.

SGML: Standard Generalized Mark-up Language. A standardized system designed to enable documents to be accessed regardless of the system in which they are created. SGML codes are applied to the elements of a document in order to identify them.

Subject files: A type of file traditionally used in a paper based filing system. Subject files consist of records that are kept together because they are about the same subject and are often filed alphabetically. Most reference files in an office are subject files.

Vital records: Records that are necessary for the day-to-day operation of an organization. The destruction of vital records would disrupt business operations. Workflow: Systems to track and automate the flow of work in an organization. Workflow software enables the steps in work to be controlled more efficiently.

Workflow: Systems to track and automate the flow of work in an organization. Workflow software enables the steps in work to be controlled more efficiently.

Index